AF405482

Mere Christianity: For Kids

Mere Christianity

For Kids

D. Joseph Remington

To Alana – our "late-in-life" surprise who has brought many blessings to her mother and me.

Table of Contents

Introduction

As a parent, I wanted to teach my seven-year-old daughter Alana about being part of the Christian Family with accountability to the congregation. To that end, I considered the various Lutheran "Small Catechisms" published in the U.S. along with some Catholic Catechisms. I also looked over the Children's Catechism used by Reformed denominations to teach children (https://reformed.org/historic-confessions/the-childrens-catechism/), along with the Larger and Lesser Catechisms from which it is derived, and I felt it could be significantly improved. For instance, in the very first two questions, it just doesn't strike me as very "natural". The whole thing seemed to me to be a series of stilted questions/answers that a child would never give except for rote memorization.

Rote memorization is the lowest form of learning in Bloom's Taxonomy of Learning (I once was a post-secondary instructor for a short time, long ago.) The first question is "Who made you?" The answer is intuitive enough, but when asked "What else did God make?" (the second question) I can see Alana try to give an itemized list, if she were asked before seeing the expected answer ("Ans: God made all things.")

The inadequacy of such catechisms for teaching the Christian Faith to children today is highlighted by some very sobering statistics. One study has shown that 40-50% of children from "good families" and involved in youth groups will drift away from God after they leave high school. Other researchers say as many as 80% of such believers will drift away from God by the age 29. And that also got me thinking about preparing Alana for adulthood in God's Family.

As someone who's actually been tested by the heathen/pagan/atheist masses, I believe the larger part of the problem is that kids today just aren't being prepared to execute St. Peter's exhortation to "be ready with answers for the reason for our hope" (**1Pt 3:15**). The issue is an unhealthy reliance on assumptions - assumptions that those outside forces won't necessarily share. For instance, how do we know God exists? "Because the Bible tells me so" isn't going to cut it when these kids run into skeptics who will tear such reasoning to philosophical shreds.

So then, I took it upon myself to come up with a more structured approach to Alana's upbringing in the Christian Family. Over the course of three months, I had a series of thirteen 5-10 minute conversations with Alana about God and Church. Since the Apostles' Creed is a summary of the essentials of the Christian Faith, I started with that as my outline. I used C.S. Lewis' approach to explaining Christianity without resorting to "proof-texts" from the Bible because I want Alana to have it "written upon her heart" (**Heb 10:16**) and not just a bunch of regurgitated memory verses. I called this series of lessons <u>Mere Christianity: *For Kids*</u> as a nod to C.S. Lewis.

Another thing I kept in mind is that right from the beginning of the Church, there were two great heresies that still crop up in some form in our modern world: 1. Gnosticism - the belief that Jesus is not really human and that there is some secret knowledge that can be learned so that we can shed this corrupt flesh and become divine (Mormonism is the big one in today's world); 2. Arianism - in the late third century, many Christians followed the teachings of Bishop Arius - that the Son is NOT eternal and was created by the Father (Jehovah's Witnesses is the big group of Arianists in today's world.)

With such competing views about the nature of Jesus, the Roman Emperor Constantine called together a synod of 300 bishops from around the empire. He summoned the bishops to the city of Nicea to work out their differences in beliefs - specifically regarding Gnosticism and Arianism. The resulting "profession of faith" of the 300 bishops is the Nicene Creed.

Back in 1985-86, I'd had several encounters with Jehovah's Witnesses, Mormons and Seventh Day Adventists. I saw firsthand how they misinterpreted the Scriptures to fit their theology. And with that in mind, I want Alana to be fully prepared and girded against such teachings as she grows into adulthood. I want her to be able to understand the concepts of Christian belief, not just memorize scripture. Therefore, I also incorporated the Nicene Creed (which is really just an expanded exposition of the Apostles' Creed) into my outline.

For her 6th birthday, I gave her a Bible - the NIrV Adventure Bible for Early Readers - which she picked out herself because of the turtle motif on the cover. It is a full Bible intended for kids ages 6-10. There are a couple of sensitive topics in the Apostles' Creed that I wanted to make sure I covered in an "age appropriate" manner. For instance, in writing the section on crucifixion, I referred to her Bible as a guide, using the wording and language which describes Jesus' crucifixion, which in reality was pretty run-of-the-mill by Roman standards. In her Bible, I found descriptions that I felt were detailed enough but written for her age. I think I've softened that section appropriately as it doesn't go into any detail that she won't find in her Bible.

When I started writing the essays about the individual articles of the Apostles' and Nicene Creed, I shared them with a select few people, looking for their feedback. One of those was an ordained minister who kept suggesting that I include proof-texts from the Bible even though I explained why I didn't intend to. He was the one who originally suggested I put the essays into a book form to be shared beyond just my family, so as a compromise I've included an appendix with those Bible references. It ended up that the appendix is just as long as the book itself.

That appendix became a "Parents' Guide" in which I've included a copy of the Apostles' Creed and the Nicene Creed. Additionally, I've provided Scripture references for each of the chapters. Again, each chapter is written as a short five-minute conversation between parent and child. Therefore I recommend that parents read all the chapters with their child first before going over the contents in the appendix. And then, while re-reading a given chapter together, review the corresponding Scripture passages that go with it. It is my fervent hope that all readers, adult and child, learn something here. God desires for everyone to genuinely seek to know him better and his will for us.

God created heaven and earth

In the beginning, there was nothing. Well, nothing that we would recognize as "something". The scientific evidence we can find shows us that the whole universe once existed as a big black hole. We don't know how long all this mass was just sitting there like that but we do know, by the evidence, that it just inexplicably exploded suddenly. In the first three minutes of that explosion, all the mass of protons, electrons and neutrons (and other matter) came into existence. This explosion is referred to as "The Big Bang".

According to the known rules of science, a body of mass at rest will stay at rest unless acted upon by an outside force. If you put a rock down on a table, the rock won't move, unless something makes it move. In the same way, a firecracker won't explode until someone lights it. You can put a firecracker on the ground and look at it all day long, but it won't explode until someone or something lights the fuse. The "someone" who started "The Big Bang" is God.

If we look closely at the world we're living in, we can see the hand of this Creator-God all around us. For instance, Bombardier beetles are ground beetles which have a unique defense they use when threatened: they squirt a hot spray from the end of their belly with a popping sound. The spray is produced from mixing two chemicals, which are stored in two reservoirs in the beetle's abdomen. When the solution reaches the spout, the two chemicals mix. Heat from the reaction brings the mixture to near the boiling point of water and produces gas that drives the ejection. The damage caused can be fatal to attacking insects. If we tried to put those two chemicals together in our bodies, we would get really hurt, but somehow the beetle is unharmed.

Egyptian plovers and Nile crocodiles have a unique symbiotic relationship. Crocodiles get food stuck in their teeth. The food rots their teeth which probably causes some pain. When it feels the need for a good tooth cleaning, the crocodile will sit with its mouth wide open. The Egyptian plover bird sees the invitation and will fly into the mouth of the crocodile, eat the food stuck in its teeth, and fly away unharmed. If we tried to put ourselves in a crocodile's mouth, we'd get eaten! Somehow, the crocodile knows not to eat the plovers.

The special relationship between clownfish and sea anemones is called symbiosis. Clownfish are the only fish that do not get stung by the tentacles of the sea anemone. They have a slimy mucus covering that protects clownfish from the sea anemone. However, if this covering is wiped off, the clownfish will get stung and possibly killed when it returns home to the anemone. The clownfish and the sea anemone help each other survive in the ocean. The clownfish, while being provided with food, cleans away fish and algae leftovers from the anemone. And the sea anemones are given better water circulation as the clownfish fan their fins while swimming about. Somehow the clownfish has the slimy covering just so it can live in the anemone and no other reason.

The lesser whitethroat (Sylvia curruca), is a small migratory bird that lives during the summer in Europe and in Africa during the winter. The lesser whitethroat breeds in temperate Europe and crosses the Sahara desert twice each year. In both crossings, adults migrate earlier than their children, leaving the younger birds to find their own way. That would be like your mom and dad leaving to go somewhere without telling you and then after they're gone, you go and meet up with them wherever they went.

Photosynthesis is a process used by plants to convert light into food that can later be released to fuel the organisms' activities. This food is stored in the form of carbohydrates, such as sugars, which are synthesized from carbon dioxide and water. Oxygen is also released as a byproduct. Although some of the steps in photosynthesis are still not completely understood, the overall process has been known since the 1800s. Even still, we can't make anything that actually does photosynthesis ourselves.

Even though we know the ingredients and how things fit together, man cannot give life. We know how cells are put together and we know how cells divide to become many more cells. We know how to keep cells alive. We know what living cells are made of but once a cell is dead, it's dead. Dead cells can't be brought back to life. We don't know how to give life to dead things. The odds of life just randomly occurring is like expecting to put a bunch of Legos in a bag, shaking the bag, and then get a Lego house when we're done shaking.

We can see the Hand of God all around us if we just keep our eyes open. In the birds who clean crocodile teeth; in the fish who help clean stinging anemones; in the young birds who find their parents who just leave them on their own; in the green plants that give us clean air to breathe.

It should stand to reason that the Creator of the world is so much bigger than the world. In fact, in order to have started the Big Bang, God had to exist outside of time and space. God has to be and is infinite. It is impossible to understand everything about God because, unlike God, we are small and finite. Because God is so big and we are so small, we only understand that which he reveals to us. It's like this: a whole box of cereal won't fit into just one bowl.

God made everything - both the visible and the invisible. So far we've talked about the things we can see – the visible. But what about the invisible? All we have to do to see the invisible is to think about what goes on in our minds. When you go to school and play with your friends, sometimes they don't do what you think is fair. Sometimes you do things to your friends that you know you shouldn't do. That's your sense of Fair Play. It's about doing what's right. You aren't told by anyone else, but you still know when you're doing the right thing. Another word for this sense of doing the right thing is your "conscience". But it's more than just instinct. Sometimes it's about doing something even though you might get hurt – like going into a burning building to help someone. Some people also call your conscience the "Moral Law".

Now then, so far we've discussed how we can see the *work* of God which shows us that he's all around us. But even though we see his handiwork, we don't actually see God. There's something that separates you from the God who made you: Sin. What exactly is sin? Sin is failing to act out of love for God or others. It's when you don't listen to your conscience to do what you know is the right thing. Sin is trying to hide ourselves from God just like when you try to hide behind your mom or dad when strangers talk to you. And so, just like you don't see strangers when you're hiding your face from them, the separation of sin keeps us from really seeing God. And the problem with sin is that everyone has it – not just you. Sin is a birth-defect we get from our parents, just like how you got your blue eyes and red hair from your mom and dad.

People who have thought a lot about what sin is believe that it comes from pride which feeds into other sins which also keep us from being with God. Pride is excessive belief in ourselves – that we don't need help when we do. Pride is also known as Vanity: where you think that you're the prettiest or smartest person when someone else may be prettier or smarter. Other sins that keep us from God are greed, envy, gluttony, anger and sloth.

Greed is the desire for more stuff when we already have plenty. Such as when we have two cookies and don't share with someone who doesn't have any. Envy is when we want what others have to the point that we're willing to take it from them or hope that they lose what they have. It's like when your friend at school has a neat toy that you take when they aren't looking – or even when they are watching. Gluttony is kind of like greed, but a bit different. While greed is when you try to keep more than you need, gluttony is taking and using more than your fair share. It's like eating two hot dogs when there's only enough for everyone to have just one or eating a piece of cake when you're not hungry. Anger, or Wrath, is when you hurt someone because you are upset. It's when you push someone down at school or call them names because you think they did something to upset you. Sloth is the avoidance of doing your chores. Sloth is when you should be picking up your toys but play games on your phone instead, or watching TV instead of doing your homework.

When God created everything, he didn't make people sinful. So what happened? Satan happened. Satan takes advantage of something God gave us and twisted it to hurt us. That something is the freedom to choose. We all have the conscience that God gives us, but we also can choose to ignore that conscience and not do the right thing. Satan uses temptation to get us to ignore our conscience and give in to sin. Temptation makes not doing the right thing look like something you want. It's like when you know you should pick up your toys because you're done playing with them, but you also know that playing games on your phone would be more fun. Being tempted is not sin: giving in to temptation is sin.

Like any parent who loves his children, God wants us to return to his family from the separation of sin. When you were born, your mom and dad kept you close because you belong in their family. Good parents love their children and try very hard to do what's best for them. And God loves everyone in the world more than that – more than your mom and dad love you. But because of the separation of sin, we can't see God except what he shows us. It's like when you hurt your dad's feelings: your mom can't be the one to make it better. Your dad needs to be the one you talk to so you can make it better with him. So it's God that has to be the one to show us the way to be with him as part of his family.

It had to be God ..

When we do something to hurt a classmate's feelings, it does no good to apologize to someone else. In order to make things right, you need to apologize to the person whose feelings you hurt, even if you didn't mean to. Sometimes we all do things that hurt others even though we don't mean to. And when that happens, we still need to do something to make it right. Sometimes, it's as simple as saying we're sorry, if we really mean it. But it's not up to us what it will take to make it right. It's up to the person who was hurt.

When we don't do the right things that we know we should do, it's God who is hurt, along with the other people who get hurt because we sinned. So it is God who has to be the one to accept our apologies. Not any angels; not your mom and dad; not your teachers – God is the only one. And the thing is God knows your heart, since he created you and your conscience. He'll know if you really mean it when you say you're sorry for not doing the right thing. And God *really, really wants* to accept our apologies when we hurt him.

Because of sin, God himself had to come in person to show us the way to overcome the separation caused by sin. He couldn't send an angel to do it, because it isn't the angels that are hurt by our sin. It had to be God. There was no other way. So that's what God did: He came down from heaven and showed us the way to overcome our sin and how to apologize for hurting him.

When we go into a dark room, we normally use some sort of light to find our way around. Sometimes we go driving when it's dark at night, or when it's raining, so I turn on the headlights to see where we're going on the road ahead. I often use a flashlight to see my path when I go walking outside at night so I don't trip over rocks and things. And like that darkness of night, because of our separation from God, we are living "in the dark". God came to us to as a light by which we find our way to him through the darkness of sin. The angels aren't the light. Nor is it somebody who says they know a shortcut from the darkness back to God. That light is God revealing himself for us to follow the path he shows us.

We call this "redemption" because we are being saved from the darkness - the separation. Since it is God who is both forgiving us and saving us, we say that he is God the Redeemer.

I said before that what we know about God is what he chooses to show us. We can't know anything else about God. One of the things that has been shown to us is that God-Creator is also God-Redeemer. God the Redeemer is the same God as God the Creator. But God the Redeemer is a "persona" or "aspect" of God that is different from God the Creator.

An aspect is how something appears from one direction. It's like the dice from one of your board games. On the die, there are dots on each side, but each side has a different number of dots. One side has one dot and another side has two dots. Two different aspects of the same die. In the same way, we have God-Creator and God-Redeemer - two different aspects but the same, one God.

Before you were born, part of your dad and part of your mom came together inside your mom and there God gave you life. And for about nine months, you grew inside your mom and then you were born. You were a person, just like your mom and your dad. We call that "begetting". You are "begotten" of your dad and mom - they are both part of you. Some creatures, like sea stars (or starfish), don't have both a mom and a dad - they have just a dad.

God made all plants and animals based on something called a "cell". A cell is like a very small Lego and it takes *billions* of cells to make your body. One cell becomes two cells by something called "mitosis". Mitosis is where a cell divides itself into two identical cells that are just like the first cell. It's kind of like that with God-Redeemer and God-Creator: God-Redeemer is begotten of God-Creator. Just like photosynthesis, we don't understand it completely, but this is what God has shown us about himself.

God-Redeemer has no resemblance to created things, but is in every respect like God-Creator who begot him. And just like cellular mitosis, where the daughter cells are identical in substance to the parent cell, God-Redeemer is identical in substance to God-Creator.

Because God-Redeemer is begotten of God-Creator, we also call God-Creator "God the Father" and God-Redeemer "God the Son". Remember how I said that God exists outside of time and space? That means that the Son has always been with the Father and always will be. The Son, being God, existed before the Big Bang; before time began. Again, we don't understand it completely, since we are three-dimensional creatures living inside time and space while God exists outside, but that is another thing God has shown us about himself.

Another thing about God the Son that it is important to understand is that he is not created. You were created. Your mom and dad were created, just like you. Your cat, Pumpkin, was created. Everything we see around us was created. The angels were created. But not God the Son. He is begotten of God the Father, but he was not created.

Since the Son and the Father are both one God, both were responsible for creating everything. We know by what God has shown us that another name for God the Son is "the Word of God." The Father spoke the Word and then everything was created. "God said" and things happened. That's why the Son is called "the first-born of creation" – because by him all things were made.

In order to reach us, the Son became one of us because our understanding of him is so limited. God's language is so complex. It isn't just sounds and phrases. In order for humans to understand the language of God, God became a human person. Think about it: God's language created everything around us. In order for us to truly understand him, the Father sent the Son, his Word, down from heaven. Jesus is God who got down to our level and became man.

On the Same Page

When grown-ups want to teach you something, they try to get to your level and explain things in a way that you already know. They work with you and often do things first and then let you try to do what they do. When teaching you to roller-skate, the grown-ups put on roller-skates too and skate with you to show you how it's done. Or think about when your mom and dad show you how to cook. We don't just stand you in front of the stove and tell you to get to it, do we? Grown-ups call this idea "being on the same page."

It's the same way with what God-Redeemer has done for us, to show us how to overcome the separation of Sin. As I said before, because of our separation from God, we can never really fully understand God. We can only see a dim shadow of him through what he reveals to us by his handiwork. He became one of us in the person of Jesus Christ. We've already talked about how Jesus is God, but he is also fully human. It may not be easy to understand, but it is what God has shown us about himself.

Do you know what a witness is? A witness is someone who saw something happen and tells what he saw. When you see someone at school do something naughty, then you are a witness and you should tell someone what you saw. When a witness tells about what they saw or know, we call that "testimony". When you give such testimony, you're supposed to tell the truth and not make things up.

One thing we've learned about telling stories about the past is that if we don't write it down, then we'll forget.

This is normal. You don't remember everything that happened when you were three years old, but when you look at pictures, then you sometimes remember - like the time you went to the zoo for your second birthday, or to Incredible Pizza for your third birthday. It's the same thing about history. You know stories about George Washington and Abraham Lincoln because witnesses wrote down what they saw.

Just as people wrote down the testimony of witnesses about the Presidents, they also wrote down the testimony about Jesus. That's how we know he is a real person. Some of the testimony was written in the Bible and some of it was written in other books. One man who wrote about Jesus, but not in the Bible, was Josephus Flavius. Another man that mentioned Jesus in his history book was Tacitus. Jesus is also mentioned in the Mishna - a group of Jewish oral stories that were written down so they won't be forgotten. But perhaps the most compelling testimony to the fact that Jesus is a real person is that he is also mentioned in the Talmud - another group of Jewish religious writings.

The testimony that we learn the most about Jesus as a real person was put in the Bible. From those witnesses we know that Jesus got hungry and thirsty. He sometimes got frustrated with his friends. There were times when he was tired. At other times, he was angry. More than once Jesus felt sorry for people who needed his help even to the point he would cry.

And just like the rest of us, Jesus was tempted by Satan to disregard God the Father's will. According to the witness testimony, Satan offered to give the entire world (which had been given to him by God the Father) to

Jesus - if Jesus would bow down to him. What Satan offered was to let Jesus off the hook so he wouldn't have to die to save us from the sins of the world. That's pretty tempting because Jesus is a person and no person in their right mind wants to die. But it would have been wrong to bow down to Satan instead of God the Father so Jesus didn't give in to the temptation.

We are told by the witnesses that Jesus is loyal to the Father above all else. Even though he is God, he set the example for us to submit ourselves to God by becoming a person like us and submitted himself to the Father to the point of dying.

Beyond all the things that show us that Jesus is a person, he is God as well. According to the witnesses, Jesus not only said he is God but he performed many miracles as signs to prove it. He healed sick people who doctors couldn't cure. He helped blind people to see. He even did something that no mere person, angel or even Satan could do: He brought dead people back to life.

Of all the miracles surrounding the life of Jesus, the very first was probably his birth. The Spirit of God entered a woman named Mary, and made a baby grow inside her. That's how Mary became Jesus' mommy. But the most surprising part to me is that Mary was a virgin. A virgin is a woman who has not shared her body with a man. Virgins don't normally become mommies, but Mary, Jesus' mother, did. It was the first sign that Jesus the man is also God-Redeemer.

How do we know that we can trust the testimony about Jesus? We know the witnesses are reliable because they were willing to die because of the testimony they told about Jesus. Would you tell a fib to your mom or dad or teacher just to get into trouble? Sometimes the stories told by the witnesses are different from each other, but that doesn't mean that someone is lying. No one sees the same event exactly the same way. Like when you went to watch the fireworks for Independence Day: there were some that you didn't get to see well because there were trees in your way. But that doesn't mean the people who were sitting on the other side of the trees were watching a different show. The other people just had a different (maybe better) point of view.

The important thing to remember here is that God became human so that we might overcome the separation of Sin. That human is Jesus Christ. And he died for us because of Sin. When the first people sinned, they brought that birth-defect to everyone. And with that birth-defect came death. Yes, every person will die eventually because sin separates us from God. Since Sin brought death to us, Jesus died to bring healing from Sin. Jesus died and showed us how to obey God's instruction: Do the right thing that our conscience tells us, no matter what.

Jesus Suffered and Died

Pontius Pilate was the governor of Judea, the Roman name for where Jerusalem is. It was his job to keep the peace and to make sure that Roman law was obeyed. The people in Judea were Jewish, but the Romans (from the city of Rome) ruled over them. Think about school, where you have the principal who is in charge of the whole school, and your teacher who is in charge of your class. The principal is like the Roman king and your teacher is like Pilate.

Remember that time you got stung by a bee? It hurt a lot, didn't it? And now, you try your best to avoid getting stung again when you see a bee or wasp. But that was just one sting by a small insect. Imagine if it were 100 bees. Or what about the time you stubbed your toe at the fireworks show on July 4th? I'm pretty sure that you're going to be more careful when running around in sandals again. Just think if you had scraped yourself all over, getting all 10 toes cut. Jesus was hurt much worse than 100 bees and getting scraped all over.

The Jewish leaders wanted to get rid of Jesus, although Pilate didn't have a good reason under Roman law to kill Jesus. But since it was his job to keep the peace, Pilate tried to calm the agitated Jewish mob and had Jesus beaten, instead of killing him. Jesus ended up with over 40 deep cuts all over his body. Pilate's soldiers took an old robe and put it on Jesus' bleeding cuts. Then when the blood dried a little bit, they ripped the robe off, like when you take a Band-aid off. This sort of beating is called "scourging". And because the Jewish leaders told the Romans that Jesus was claiming to be their king, the soldiers further made fun of Jesus and hurt him by making a crown from a small wreath with long, very sharp thorns.

Getting beaten wasn't good enough for the Jewish leaders. They wanted Jesus to die so he'd stop causing trouble for them. Many of the Jews were afraid that the Romans would hurt them if Jesus didn't stop stirring things up. They figured it would be better that one man should die instead of hundreds - which the Roman soldiers had done in other places. So after they kept nagging at Pilate, he gave in and had the Roman soldiers execute Jesus by crucifixion along with two criminals.

We know from many historical records that the Roman soldiers had crucifying people down to a science. Crucifixion is a method of execution in which the prisoner is tied or nailed to a large wooden cross and left to hang, until eventual death from exhaustion and asphyxiation. Asphyxiation means air is taken away so you can't breath. Death by crucifixion was intended to be slow, humiliating, painful, and public.

Crucifixion was carried out by teams consisting of a commanding centurion and his soldiers. First, the prisoner would be scourged with a leather whip which had sharp pieces of bone or metal near the ends. This made their back bleed so much that they sometimes died. The prisoner then usually had to carry the horizontal beam to the place of execution, but not necessarily the whole cross.

The prisoner would be led through the most crowded streets bearing a sign proclaiming the prisoner's name and crime (a titulus). At the place of execution, the prisoner had any clothing taken away and then was nailed to the cross. The hands would be nailed to the cross first, then the feet or ankles. The titulus would then be fastened to the cross as the prisoner hung there.

Roman guards could leave the site only after the prisoner had died, so sometimes they brought death quicker by deliberately breaking the legs, stabbing into the heart with a spear, sharp blows to the front of the chest, or a smoking fire built at the foot of the cross to asphyxiate the victim. The Romans usually forbade burial. The bodies of the crucified were typically left on the crosses to decompose and be eaten by animals.

According to the witness statements, all of this happened to Jesus. Except, according to the testimony, there was an earthquake when Jesus died, and the soldiers wanted to get out of there, so they were going to kill all three victims being crucified. After they saw Jesus was already dead, because of the water that came out when he was stabbed with a spear, the soldiers didn't bother breaking his legs.

Because of the earthquake, the Romans even declared aloud that Jesus was "a son of a god" (Romans at the time believed there were many gods.) And because a rich man named Joseph of Arimathea asked, the Romans also let Jesus' friends take his body down from the cross before any animals ate him. It was this same Joseph of Arimathea that gave his own tomb so Jesus could be buried, instead of being left outside to rot. Tombs like that were cut into rocky hillsides. A large round stone was rolled in front of the opening to close it after Jesus was put in it.

By dying, Jesus provided the sacrifice needed to overcome our own sinful nature. Sin brought death into the world and so death removes sin. Could sin have been overcome some other way than dying? I don't know, but God does. I can only assume that if there were a better way, God would have gone that route.

What if Jesus hadn't died? Jesus didn't have to die. He chose to die. For us. For you. God the Son submitted himself to the will of God the Father. But what if he hadn't? What if he had given in to the temptation of Satan and bowed down to him in the desert? Then he would have proven Satan to be wiser than God.

Remember Satan? Jesus saw him fall from heaven with 1/3 of all the angels. The angels were right there in the very presence of God. They knew God in all his glory, and yet many of them turned away. If Jesus hadn't died, then no one would turn back to God, just like the fallen angels refused to turn back to God, because Satan would be seen as wiser and greater than God.

Jesus became man specifically to die and thereby break open the gates to the underworld. When Jesus lived with us, he did and said a lot of things to show us that he is God. But he became man to help us turn from Sin and bring us back to God. And as I already said, God determined that dying was the way to make that happen. But Jesus didn't die just for the people living back then, and he didn't die just for the people like you who have been born since then. He also died to save those who went to the grave before him. He died to save everyone whose heart was turned from their own sinful nature.

To Hell and Back

Ever since the first people sinned, God has wanted us to overcome the separation brought by that sin. He even became man, in the person of Jesus, to help us; to show us the way. But Jesus didn't come just to save you and me. Jesus came into the world as a man to save everyone, including those who had already died. So what did he do to reach out to the people who died before he was born - those who didn't have a chance to hear him?

After he died on the cross, he went to where the dead souls are held in a sort of waiting room. A waiting room is a place where people sit and wait - like at the doctor's office. The Greek word for the waiting room is "Hades" while the Hebrew word is "Sheol". In English, we call that waiting-place "Hell", but it's not the same as the place of "eternal punishment". It's like that with the word "fork" - you can have a fork that you eat with or you can have a fork in the road (where you have a choice to go more than one way.) We also call it "Place of the Dead", the "Underworld," or the "Grave."

Remember how I mentioned that God exists beyond time and space? He even gave himself the name "I AM" to explain it to us. That means that God is here yesterday, today *and* tomorrow, all at once. It is the same way for Heaven where God dwells. There is no passage of time in Heaven because it is a place outside of time. And it is the same for the Underworld.

The whole reason Jesus went into the world of the dead was to lead them out of the darkness into the Light. It's the same exact reason that Jesus became man in the first place. God the Son - God-Redeemer - came to bring redemption from sin to all mankind, living and dead. God is a Loving Father who wants to be reconciled with all of his creation. It seems only fitting to me that God-Redeemer would reach out to those who didn't have the opportunity in life to know about Jesus.

We're told by the witnesses that while Jesus was dead and buried, when he went to the place where the dead souls are kept, he preached to the dead and freed them from the separation of sin. He declared victory over Satan. In declaring victory, Jesus broke down the gates separating the Underworld from Heaven and broke the chains of the souls who had not ignored their conscience and rejected God - rejected Jesus.

Now Jesus could have gone straight back to Heaven where he came from after freeing all the souls from the Underworld. But what kind of message would that have left for us here on Earth? Without Jesus rising from the grave, then we'd have no hope because then there would not have been the victory over death - the separation of sin. Jesus would have been seen as simply a man who had said and done some interesting things. But according to the witness testimony, on the third day after dying on the cross, Jesus did come back to life. He did it to complete the message that he started teaching us in the first place.

Was Jesus the first person to be raised from the dead? No. Jesus himself had brought a few people back to life after they died. There was his friend, Lazarus; a little girl; and a son of a Roman soldier. But the difference between them and Jesus is that they would all die again but Jesus died only once. It was when Jesus rose from the dead that he brought the gift of the resurrection to all of us - not just a few. Jesus is also called "Firstborn from the dead" because his resurrection is the most important.

At first, after his resurrection, Jesus revealed himself only to a few of his closest friends. And even though they had known him for over three years, they still didn't recognize him at first! The fact that they saw him die was very hard on them - so hard that it was almost impossible for them to accept that Jesus is alive again. That's probably why Jesus chose to show himself only to a few close friends. If he had shown himself to the whole world, then everybody would have likely thought it was some sort of trick, like he was a ghost or something.

But it wasn't a trick. We know from the witness statements that Jesus walked along with his discouraged friends on long hikes. He even ate with them. When was the last time you heard of a ghost or spirit walking with their feet or eating actual food?

Not only was Jesus not a ghost, he had the *same* body that he had before he died! If he had a different body, then that would have been what is called "reincarnation." Jesus was resurrected - not reincarnated. To be reincarnated would not have proved that Jesus is the almighty God, able to defeat Satan. Jesus showed that he is God, and that as God, he had power over life *and* death. But how do we know that Jesus had the same body? Because the witnesses tell us that he still had the scars from being crucified.

Thomas was one of Jesus' close friends. When the others

told him that they had seen Jesus alive again, he didn't believe them at first. Thomas said that he wouldn't believe them until he saw the holes in Jesus' hands and feet. So what did Jesus do? According to the witness statements, Jesus showed Thomas the holes in his hands and feet as well as the hole in his side where he was stabbed with the spear. Jesus even invited Thomas to touch the scars so he might know for certain that it really was Jesus, in the flesh.

After Jesus was resurrected, he spent time with his friends and followers helping them get ready for the rough times ahead. He taught them a bit more about the Kingdom of God - Heaven. He told them what he had done for the souls held in the Underworld. For 40 days, he was with them and when he felt they were ready, he went back to Heaven. He told them that he was leaving to be with the Father, preparing the way for them to join him later. It's like when your mom and dad get your house ready for when visitors come over to stay. Only Jesus went back to Heaven to get his house ready for us to stay forever.

King of the World

So if Jesus was resurrected from the dead and he only died once, where is he now? We can't see him and have conversations with him like we can with presidents, kings and queens. Since he's nowhere on Earth to be found, Jesus must be somewhere else. What gives?

Remember your school field trips to the Memphis Zoo and Mud Island? There were guides to show your class around and tell about the interesting things to see. It's kind of like that with what Jesus did. The entire reason for Jesus becoming human in the first place was to get down on our level to show us the way to overcome the separation of sin from God. If he'd simply stayed on Earth after being resurrected, the task would have been left undone. So, shortly after his resurrection, he finished what he started. Jesus returned to Heaven so that we would be guided by him like when you were following the guide at the zoo.

What would have happened if Jesus didn't go back to Heaven? I think that most people would not recognize him as being God. Remember Satan? Even he, being in the very presence of God at the time of creation, refused to swallow his pride and acknowledge Jesus as Lord God. It is much harder for people who have never seen God to recognize Jesus as God. There also would be no way for anyone to have a place in Heaven, if Jesus didn't go and make room for us. It's like when you ride the bus to school - if there's not a seat for you to sit, you can't go on the bus.

Do you remember what a witness is? Someone who sees something happen and tells about it is a witness. When you see someone at school do something naughty, then you are a witness. Testimony is what we call it when a witness tells about what they saw or know. And remember, when you give testimony, you're supposed to tell the truth and not make things up. We also call such testimony a "witness statement."

According to the witness statements of people who were there, after Jesus was resurrected, he spent 40 days with his friends and followers, helping them get ready to spread the good news about what he'd done. He taught them more about the Kingdom of God. Also, Jesus told them what he had done for the souls held in Hades. Jesus was going back to prepare a place with God in Heaven for them to join him later. It's like when your house is ready for when visitors come over to stay for a short visit. Except Jesus went back to Heaven to get his house ready for us to stay forever.

Being God, Jesus knows us better than we know ourselves. He explained to his friends that he had to go so that the Holy Spirit could finish teaching them what he started. He told his friends that they weren't ready to learn everything he wanted to teach them, but the Holy Spirit would guide and make them ready. It's like when your mom and dad taught you how to read. First, we started with the letters of the Alphabet and then taught you some smaller words. Then you learned bigger words as you got older. When we taught you simple math, first we taught you that $1+1=2$.

One of the most important reasons for Jesus' ascension was to make room so that the Holy Spirit could infill, strengthen and empower the Church. It requires strength greater than our own to testify for Christ. Think about how you don't like to stand up in front of everyone by yourself and sing or read. Yet, the most important chore of the Church is to be a visible witness for the invisible Kingdom of God. And we can only do that through the strength from the Holy Spirit.

How was Jesus' leaving good for the Church? While Jesus was walking the Earth in the body of a man, he was limited by space and time and he couldn't be with each one of his followers all at once. If he had stayed on earth confined to his human body, he couldn't have been there simultaneously for Peter in Rome, James in Jerusalem and Thomas in India. But the Holy Spirit can be. The Holy Spirit is God which means the Holy Spirit's presence is limitless.

The empowering presence of the Holy Spirit is with all of Jesus' followers everywhere around the world at the same time. The Holy Spirit is with your grandma down in Mississippi at the same time that he is with your other grandma in Iowa, just like the Holy Spirit is with both you *and* your mom even when you're far away from her. And that fits the whole reason that Jesus came to us in the first place: to reach out to all of mankind and help everyone overcome the separation of sin from God.

Jesus may not be visibly present with us now as he was with his friends, but he is present in our lives more than we can possibly imagine. Through dying on the cross, he fulfilled the old agreement with his own blood. And because it is now fulfilled, we are no longer obligated by the old tenets. By going back to Heaven, Jesus showed us that he rules with supreme authority. And by that authority - God's authority - Jesus has ratified a new covenant between God and man.

The terms of that new agreement are simple: Love God with all our heart, and love others as we love ourselves - treating others as we would like them to treat us. In other words, do everything with charity and kindness in your heart. To act out of pride, without charity, is to reject God - to sin.

Even though Jesus isn't here in the flesh with us now, one day he will be again. Jesus will set all things right and gather us close to him forever. When Jesus does come back, the darkness brought by sin will lift and this age of death and destruction will be over for good. Everything sad will be undone.

We are told by the witnesses that as Jesus returned to Heaven a cloud hid him from their sight. According to their testimony, they were told by angels that Jesus, who has been taken from us into Heaven, will come back in the same way that they saw him go.

The Grand Finale

As I've said before, when someone who sees something happen and tells about it, they are a witness. And when a witness tells about what they saw or know, that's what we call testimony. Remember, when you give testimony, you're supposed to tell the truth and not make things up. Jesus' friends who were with him during his time on Earth were witnesses to his life.

According to their witness testimony, when Jesus ascended back to Heaven, he promised that he will come back in the same way that they saw him go. That means that he will come in Glory and no one will miss it. There will be a great noise announcing his return, just like when we hear jet planes landing at an airport. Only this will be louder and more visible and everyone around the world will know it. It will be an awesome thing to see - bigger and brighter than even the best fireworks show.

What will Jesus do when he comes back? Why will he come back? When Jesus went back to Heaven, there were still some things left unfinished here on Earth. There are still a lot of bad things happening in the world and Jesus will make all those things right. He will gather those who accept his commandments in their heart to be close to him forever. When Jesus does come back, the darkness brought by sin will lift. There won't be any more death and destruction. Everything sad will be undone.

When will that happen? I don't know. Nobody does. Although, there have been quite a few people who have claimed that they knew exactly when Jesus would return. And they were all wrong. Some said that they had been told by angels, or God himself. They weren't. Others have said that they were able to figure out secret messages written in the Bible. But still they were wrong.

Why have so many people gotten it wrong? The fact is that Jesus himself told his friends that only the Father knows when Jesus will return. Not the angels - so how can they tell anyone? Not the Son or the Holy Spirit - so how can they tell anyone? The point of God the Father keeping such knowledge to only himself is to keep us on our toes. Most people when they have a deadline will put things off until the last minute like when you study for your spelling test. God doesn't want us to wait to the last minute to become followers of Jesus.

However, the sad fact is that Satan is still out in the world, deceiving many people. There have been some of those who have falsely claimed to be sent by God. And until Jesus comes again, there will always be more such people. But how do we know that such people are not sent by God? Because Jesus promised us two things: 1. He himself would come back in glory; and 2. The person sent by God is the Holy Spirit who is invisible without a physical body.

Now what about all the bad things we hear about on the news: hurricanes, tornadoes, earthquakes, climate change, wars? Don't those things mean Jesus is coming really soon? No. I'm afraid not. Jesus even told his friends that those sort of things were only the beginning of the troubles that would happen until he comes back from Heaven. There has been and will continue to be great trouble in the world like wars and natural disasters.

Don't be afraid though. Jesus did give us one hint about what to look for when the time of his return gets near. Jesus said that he will return after the Good News about his story has been told to every country around the world. The Holy Spirit will have completed her mission and every living person on Earth will have had a chance to hear the story of Jesus.

Once Jesus does come back, he will gather everyone together who accepted him into their heart and followed his example. As for the people who are selfish and don't help those who need help, they are the ones who Jesus will send to the place of eternal torment. That's the place where they will be chained forever, away from God's presence. It will be like putting you in timeout forever and never letting you see your mom or dad ever again.

Remember what I said about pride? Pride is the excessive belief in ourselves – that we never need help and that we're better than everyone else. Pride is also known as vanity and it is really the sin that leads to all other sins. The people that Jesus will put in eternal timeout are the people who rejected the Holy Spirit out of pride and do things their own selfish way.

Who is the the Holy Spirit? We've discussed the first person, or aspect, of God: God-Creator or God the Father. Also, we've discussed the second person, or aspect, of God: God-Redeemer or God the Son. The Holy Spirit is the third aspect of God. Remember, an aspect is how something appears from one direction. One side of a cube is one aspect, but it is not the whole cube. So the Holy Spirit is God just as Jesus is God.

While the Father, Son and Holy Spirit are all one God, it is important to remember there's an important distinction between them. When we think or say something bad about God the Father, God will forgive us. If we think or say something bad about God the Son, Jesus, he will forgive us. But rejecting the Holy Spirit is the only sin that will not be forgiven.

When I first learned this, it kind of scared me. How do you know if you've rejected the Holy Spirit? If you're asking the question, then you haven't rejected her. It's the people who've rejected the Holy Spirit that won't care. In fact they might even get very upset if you try to tell them about Jesus.

But don't let that get you down. Some people might be having a bad day. Some people might be having a bad life. The important thing for you is to keep on trying to let the Holy Spirit guide you to follow Jesus. As long as you do that, you'll be fine.

The Friendly Ghost

Who is the the Holy Spirit? So far, we know God-Creator or God the Father is the first person of God. We also know that God-Redeemer or God the Son is the second person of God. The Holy Spirit is the third person of God. The Holy Spirit is God just as Jesus is God. But the Holy Spirit is not the same person as Jesus or the Father.

While the human body of Jesus was limited by time and space, the empowering presence of the Holy Spirit is everywhere around the world all at once. The Holy Spirit is with both you *and* your mom even when you're far away from her. And that's what God has planned all along: to reach out to all of mankind and help everyone overcome the separation of sin from God.

The Holy Ghost isn't like the ghosts or phantoms we see in movies or read about in books. She isn't trying to haunt or harm us. In fact, the Holy Spirit is trying to bring us closer to God by telling us what Jesus and the Father want us to learn from him. It is a quiet voice that we hear with our minds, not our ears. But to hear it, sometimes we need to be quiet and listen close. Other times, it's like we can't hear or think about anything else but the one thought that Holy Spirit puts into our head.

Just like God the Son, the Holy Ghost comes from God the Father. But unlike God the Son, God the Spirit doesn't have a physical body that we can see or touch. That doesn't mean that the Spirit can't touch us, because she does touch us inside. If we open our mind to her, she prods us to follow the path that Jesus sets before us. It's like when your mom and dad hold your hand when crossing a street or walking in a parking lot.

We are expected to worship the Holy Spirit but only because the Holy Spirit is God. We aren't supposed to worship angels, other people, or the things they make - only God. Jesus described the Spirit as a "comforter". That is, the Spirit is God who gives us hugs when we need it. And for that, we should give thanks and praise to God the Spirit.

God-Creator didn't create or make God the Spirit. The Holy Spirit is co-eternal with the Father and the Son which means that she also exists outside of time and space. She has always been with the Father and the Son. Even at the moment of creation, the Holy Spirit was there with the Holy Creator and the Holy Word. It is only because the Spirit is God that she is able to guide us into communion with the Creator and Redeemer.

There are two ways that the God the Spirit communicates, or speaks, to us: directly and indirectly. When the Holy Spirit breathes God's Word into our minds and thereby guides us, that is communicating with us directly. When the Holy Spirit reveals God's Word to us through the world around us or through other people, that is indirect communication. One way the Holy Spirit speaks to us indirectly is through people called prophets. A prophet is a spokesperson for God. They tell others what the Creator or Redeemer, through the Holy Spirit, has told them to say.

When listening to prophets, however, you have to be careful that the message is really from God. There have been, and always will be, some false prophets who claim mistakenly that their message comes from the Holy Spirit when it didn't. The way to tell is if the message is untrue at all. If it's not 100% true, then the message is not from God. If a prophet makes a prediction of the future that doesn't come true, then it's not from God. Don't listen to that person about anything.

Remember how you told me that it was a bit confusing to you to hear songs on the radio being played more than once, but the singer only sang the song one time? It's the same with the Holy Spirit bringing the redemption of Jesus' death to all. Jesus died only once, but by the power of the Spirit, that death is brought into all believers, so that God's grace washes over everyone.

As the Holy Spirit works through all people calling them to do God's will, she is nudging them to hear what Jesus, God-Redeemer, has done for them. There is no way for us to accept the sacrifice of Jesus except the Holy Spirit shows us. Our conscience, our sense of right and wrong, comes from the Holy Spirit. As I said before when talking about seeing God's work in the World, your sense of Fair Play - of doing the right thing - is how we know God exists at all. And that knowledge comes from the Holy Spirit.

It is through the Holy Spirit that God writes his Word on your heart. Why? When Jesus went back to Heaven, there was so much more that he wanted us to know, but we weren't ready. So now the Holy Spirit who is inside us teaches us what the Father and the Son want us to know. She doesn't teach us with a loud voice like thunder but with a quiet voice like the fluttering of butterfly wings.

Only by the Holy Spirit are we led to follow Jesus. How does that happen if the Holy Spirit is not in us *before* we accept Christ as savior? The Spirit works through both the saved and the unsaved, just as the rain falls on the undeserving as well as the deserving but that doesn't mean that everyone is saved. In order for those who are not saved to reject the Holy Spirit (the only unforgivable sin) then the Holy Spirit has to be there to be rejected.

Speaking or thinking badly of the Father, our Creator, is a sin. Speaking or thinking badly of the Son, our Redeemer, is also a sin. But those sins will be forgiven if we ask God. But when we speak or think badly of the Holy Spirit, rejecting her, that sin won't be forgiven. We talked about that before. It is the only unforgivable sin. How do you know if you've rejected the Holy Spirit? Like I said before, if you're asking the question, then you haven't rejected her. It's the people who've rejected the Holy Spirit that won't care and won't ask.

When we accept the saving grace of Jesus through the Holy Spirit, we become adopted members of God's family. It would be impossible for everyone in God's family to gather into one place all at one time, so the Holy Spirit guides us to gather together into smaller groups we call churches. In those churches, we learn more about God, have the chance to worship him with other followers of Jesus, and are better able to find ways to serve God by helping others. Church is the place where rejoicing and giving thanks to God becomes easy.

All in the Family

There's an old saying that two heads are better than one. That means it is easier for two people who help each other to solve a problem than it is for one person to solve a problem alone. It is easier for one person to go "off-track" than it is for many people, just as it's harder to break a rope of many strands than it is to break just one strand. Besides that, being lonely is a very sad feeling. People aren't meant to be alone. I think it is for that reason that God created the idea of "family".

When we accept the saving grace of Jesus through the Holy Spirit, we become adopted members of God's family. It would be impossible for everyone in God's family to gather into one place all at one time, so the Holy Spirit guides us to gather together into smaller groups we call Church congregations. In those congregations, we learn more about God, have the chance to worship him with other followers of Jesus, and are better able to find ways to serve God by helping others. Church is the place where rejoicing and giving thanks to God becomes easy.

Even though congregations may differ from each other in the way they worship and praise God, they are still part of the same family of God. Just like you are different from your mom and your mom is different from your dad. We are still part of your family, even though we are all different from each other. The most important thing is that all true congregations accept God-Redeemer, Jesus Christ, as the head of the Church, through the guiding help of God the Holy Spirit.

The main reason that people become members of a particular congregation is to gather together for prayer and worship of God in a way that touches their heart. While different congregations of the true Church may have different ways to worship God, they all have a few things in common. Every gathering for worship throughout all the congregations of the true Church will have Adoration, Confession, Thanksgiving and Supplication. Most congregations will also recite The Lord's Prayer together.

When we see how magnificent and awesome the world around us is, our hearts naturally turn to adoration for the God who created the universe. That's the whole reason God created you - so that you can enjoy living in the world and be thankful to the one who created it. When you worship God, your worries and cares of the moment will seem less important as you realize how amazing God is and how much he loves you. Adoration of God reminds us of who he is and of who it is that loves and cares for us.

When you realize how big God is, you become aware of how small you are. You realize that you have not lived as you could have done. No one can by themselves. Remember, sin is when we don't act from love for God or others, and because of sin, we all have let others down, let ourselves down, but mostly importantly, we have let God down.

In confession, you talk to God about these things, asking for his forgiveness. We all flub things; we all fail; we all fall. Talking to God about our flaws is comforting and relaxing. There is no need to pretend because God loved us before we were born and knows all our faults. God is merciful and God forgives us no matter how many times we fail, when we are truly sorry.

Thanksgiving is joyous praise of God. Gratitude and joy are closely related. When you have cuddle-time with your mom and ask her for more cuddles later, that shows your gratitude to your mom for spending time being close to you. It makes your mom feel good and it makes you feel good. When we think about what God has done - for us, for others, or throughout history - and think about receiving his forgiveness for our sins, then giving thanks is a very natural thing to do.

Supplication is when we ask God for what we need. Sometimes, supplication is requesting for God to do something, either for yourself or somebody else. God is a loving father who cares for you very much. So don't be afraid to ask God for help when you're worried or upset about something. He will always make sure that you have what you need. But remember, just because you want something doesn't mean you need it. God will always work things out in your best interest. And sometimes, just talking to God about things is help enough.

As I said, most congregations say something called the "Lord's Prayer" or the "Our Father." According to Jesus' friends, he taught them this prayer as a simple way to talk to God. It has all the parts of worship that I just talked about: Adoration, Confession, Thanksgiving and Supplication. There is a real comfort from the Holy Spirit in knowing that God's family everywhere is praying together as one person, united by words which sum up the whole Gospel.

As you've gotten older, your relationship with your mom and dad has changed. When you were a baby, you stayed at home with your mom. But now, you get up in the morning and go to school by yourself. When you were younger, you couldn't get dressed by yourself. Now you only need a little help sometimes with buttons and snaps - and tying your shoes.

In the same way, God's family has come to understand God differently over time. God hasn't changed, but the Church's understanding of him has. A lot. When Jesus went back to Heaven, he told his friends that they still had a lot to learn. And as time has gone on, the Holy Spirit has taught us those things God wants us to know to be more like Jesus.

That's why Jesus also told his friends that they needed to be ready to change their expectations of how believers are supposed to behave. It's something called the "Power of the Keys". It is through the Holy Spirit that God's family learns to see injustice where it first saw justice. It is through the "Power of the Keys" that the Church teaches all believers what the Holy Spirit reveals.

A long time ago, people accused of being witches were killed because the Church believed that God wanted witches to be killed. They believed that is what the Bible says. Because of this belief, a woman named Alice Lake was hanged in Massachusetts for being a witch nearly 400 years ago. Why did they believe she was a witch? She saw her child who had died as a baby in a dream. The good news for the Church is that because of the Power of the Keys, and through the revelation of the Holy Spirit, we no longer kill people accused of being witches.

Remember Abraham Lincoln? He was the President who stood up to end slavery in the United States. When Lincoln was younger, he saw nothing wrong with slavery. But Lincoln was convinced by the Holy Spirit to speak out against slavery. However, when Lincoln was president there were some Church leaders who believed that God approved of slavery. Deceived by Satan, they taught that God never condemned slavery in the Bible. But because the Holy Spirit opened their eyes to the truth, other Christian leaders taught that even though the Bible didn't say anything against slavery, it was still wrong. Because of the Power of the Keys, and through the revelation of the Holy Spirit, slavery is now known to be unchristian.

Jesus was killed on a cross. He was killed by the government. In some states in the United States (but not all states), people who are accused of doing very bad things, like murder or kidnapping, are killed by the government as punishment - it's called the "death penalty". A long time ago, leaders of God's family also had people killed by the government.

But now, many Christians see this is wrong because Jesus, God-Redeemer, said that the person without sin should do the killing. Therefore, they feel that Jesus said the government should never kill people as punishment.

It is because of the Power of the Keys, and through the revelation of the Holy Spirit, that we see that the death penalty as unjust. But not every Church leader in our country agrees with that because the Apostle Paul wrote that God gives the authority to the government to punish for breaking the law. Such Church leaders forget the fact that the men and women carrying out that authority sometimes make mistakes. They don't really care that the government can't give life back to someone they've killed by mistake.

By the Power of the Keys, the way we worship God is different from the way believers worshiped God long ago. Through the continuing revelation of the Living God through the Holy Spirit, God's family understands him better and is closer to what he wants us to be than long ago. But while the Power of the Keys has allowed the Church to change as the Holy Spirit guides us, one thing that has remained the same from the beginning is that baptism tells the world that we are members of God's family.

One Baptism

The way we worship God today is different from the way believers worshiped God long ago. God's family understands him better and is closer to what he wants us to be than long ago. But as the Holy Spirit guides the Church to the perfect understanding of Jesus, one thing that has remained the same from the beginning of the Church is that baptism is the sign that we are members of God's family.

When God made his promise to Abraham, circumcision became the symbol of being included in that promise for the children of Abraham - God's chosen family. It was important that all of Abraham's family become part of God's family. God even told him to have all the baby boys circumcised when they were just eight days old. That's why Jesus was circumcised when he was just a baby - because he is a descendant of Abraham.

Just as circumcision was the symbol of people becoming part of God's family as children of Abraham, baptism symbolizes being adopted into God's family as Christians. The Holy Spirit tells us outright that baptism is the sign of the promise to all Christians and their children. We are told by the friends of Jesus that when the Church first started growing that entire households were all baptised at the same time. Just like when the entire family of Abraham was circumcised when God first made his promise to Abraham.

Baptism has replaced circumcision as the sign of adoption into God's family. It follows that since babies were circumcised then that children should be baptised now. There was no requirement for babies to wait to be circumcised except that their mommy and daddy were already part of God's family. At no time has God ever said that children should not be baptised. Jesus even told his friends that children are part of God's family.

In most congregations of God's family, children are baptised when they are still babies. In others, they wait to baptise children until they are at least 12 years old. Even further, some believers don't get baptised until they are very old. The reason for waiting is usually to make sure the person being baptised is ready.

Neither Jesus nor the Holy Spirit ever said anything about being prepared as a requirement for baptism. But there is a tendency by people to add things to what God has commanded, because otherwise things seem too easy which seems to be the case for delayed baptisms.

Not only is baptism by water the sign of adoption into God's family, water baptism also illustrates baptism of the Holy Spirit. We are told by God that the Holy Spirit is "poured out" onto all of God's family. Imagine the pouring of the Holy Spirit being like when I pour water over your head when I wash your hair. Except, your eyes didn't hurt from soap when God poured his Spirit over you.

The word "baptise" comes from a Greek word that actually means "to wash". Think about that. How do you wash clothes? How do you wash dishes? How do you wash your face and hands? That's what baptism by the Spirit does to us; it washes away our sinful nature – the birth-defect that separates us from God.

There are mainly two ways that congregations of God's family actually baptise. One is called "affusion," which means "to pour." It is a reflection of how we wash hands or how the Spirit is poured out onto you. The other way is called "immersion," which means "dunked into the water." Neither Jesus nor the Holy Spirit has said anything about baptising one way or the other. But I will say that God has told us to be good stewards of his creation and baptising by pouring saves on the water we drink.

If we aren't baptised with water, we will still go to heaven if we accept the leadership of Jesus into our heart. This is because it is the baptism of God the Spirit that is most important. The baptism of the Spirit happens in our heart as God himself wills it. It is by the baptism of the Spirit that our hearts become circumcised spiritually, opening ourselves further to God in our heart.

There is nothing you could possibly do to stop being part of daddy's family or mommy's family. In the same way, there is nothing you can do to hurt God so badly that he will "un-adopt" you from his family. This is what Jesus himself told his friends, and they in turn have told us. What this means for you is that when you get baptised there will never be a reason for you to be baptised again. One baptism is sufficient for God's grace on you.

To bring forgiveness of sins to everybody was the reason that Jesus became human. Remember how I said that Jesus is called the "Firstborn of the Resurrection"? It isn't because Jesus was the first ever to be raised from the dead. He is called "Firstborn" because his resurrection is the most important. In the same way baptism is the first act symbolizing the forgiveness of sins - first because it is the most important.

You learned to pray before you were baptised. You even learned to read your Bible beforehand. Those are also important in learning to ask God to forgive sins. But the most important act in seeking forgiveness from God (absolution) is water baptism which gives a picture of the baptism by the Spirit.

The Forgiveness of Sin

The reason that Jesus became man was to bring salvation to all mankind through the forgiveness of sins. That's all well and good to say, but what does it mean? Remember that the reason God created us is so that we might be united with him in his family so that we can enjoy his creation and be thankful for it. But because of sin, we are separated from God. However, Jesus came to take the penalty for sin in our place, so that we can have forgiveness from God.

But what exactly is sin? Some say that sin is when we think, do or say something bad. But sin is much more than that. Sin is failing to act out of love for God or others. When we don't help someone who really needs help, then we've sinned against God. God commanded us to love each other more than we love ourselves. Like when we buy a meal at a restaurant for someone who is digging in the garbage dumpster at a grocery store. Don't get me wrong - God only wants us to help as we are able. If we don't have anything to give to someone in need, that's not a sin. But most people do have something they can give.

"Sin" is an English word for a Greek word that means "without witness". In addition to being failure to act out of love, sin is not giving witness of God's love for us. What does this mean? Remember, a witness is someone who tells others about what they know or saw. So, when we stay silent about what God has done, then we have sinned. Everyone in God's family is called to give witness statements, or testimony, about God.

It used to be that when something bad happened to someone that people thought it was because they sinned. Or when something good happened to them, that it was because they had done something good to be rewarded. Some people think that way still today. But the truth is that bad things happen to good people just as good things happen for bad people. A person born blind or deaf is not born that way because of sin, just as a hateful person doesn't win a prize because hate is a good thing. Remember, the rain falls on everyone - the deserving and the undeserving.

A long time ago, God's family used to remove sin from the congregation by using something called a "scapegoat". Once a year, the priest of God would select a goat and symbolically place the sins of people on the goat's head. Then that goat would be pushed out into the wild to die - away from its family and herd. In the same way, Jesus becomes our scapegoat by dying on the cross. When we are sorry for our sins and ask God to forgive us, he removes the sin from us and puts it on Jesus as he is killed on the cross.

God wants everyone to return to him and get past the separation of sin. Because of that, God is more gracious than any person and will forgive any and all of our sins - except one. Do you remember what that sin is? We talked about it when we talked about the Holy Ghost. The only kind of sin that won't be forgiven by God is when we reject and ignore God the Spirit. All other sins will be forgiven if we ask, even if we say or think bad things about God the Father or about God the Son.

Due to human nature, many people make forgiveness of sin more difficult than God intends. According to such people, acts of penance are needed to show God that we are really sorry for sins that we've committed. But requiring such things is like saying that God doesn't know our hearts when he does. Being forgiven by God doesn't have to be hard. It really is as simple as being sorry for our sins and asking God to forgive us.

When Jesus was killed on the cross, that's just what one of the other men who was being crucified with him did. He asked Jesus to remember him in Heaven because he was sorry in his heart for his sins. And Jesus forgave his sins right then and there. All the thief on the cross did was ask and he was forgiven because God knew his heart.

Sometimes people do things that hurt us. When that happens we need to be ready to forgive such hurts because we want God to forgive us for hurting him. Medical science has proven that staying angry when we get hurt causes stress and anxiety and will make us sick. It's like we let the person who hurt us to keep on hurting us. Forgiving others actually helps us change our hearts to stop sinning against God.

Even though keeping anger inside is not good for us, forgiveness is the hardest thing and goes against our natural inclinations. The plain truth is that we can't do it without help from the Holy Spirit. It is only by listening to that quiet voice of God, which gives us our conscience, that we can let go of our anger towards those who hurt us and forgive them for causing us pain. God will always answer our prayers to help us forgive others, but it still won't be easy. That's because our own sinful nature, our pride, makes it hard.

We need to forgive those who hurt us even when they don't tell us they're sorry. And sometimes, some people will keep on hurting us even after saying they're sorry. When that happens, it doesn't mean that they're not sorry. Sometimes, when people hurt us again after saying they're sorry, it's because their brains work differently from ours. Like your friends who can't sit still and have a hard time paying attention during school. They don't mean to cause trouble, but they just can't help it.

When Jesus became our scapegoat, he not only brought forgiveness for our sins, he paid the price for that forgiveness, instead of us. He didn't have to do that, but God wants us to overcome sin and live with him in Heaven. Jesus paid the ransom for our sins so that we don't have to. So there are two things we can do about that. We can either accept Jesus' payment on our behalf, or if we don't accept Jesus' payment for our sins, then we must pay the penalty ourselves.

What exactly is the penalty for sin? The way many people have described the penalty is the second death. This is different from when people get old or sick and then die. The second death will be like being put on timeout away from your mommy and daddy forever. If someone rejects Jesus' payment, they will suffer the separation of sin for eternity - never uniting with God.

So then, one thing we can be sure of is that everyone will appear before God in judgment when Jesus returns. How we end up spending eternity depends on whether we have forgiveness for our sins or not. We will all be resurrected at the day of Judgment when Jesus comes back and if we are forgiven by God for our sins, then we will be forever in God's presence as joyful members of his family. For those who don't have that forgiveness, they will be put in timeout forever, separated from God and his family.

The Resurrection of the Body

The whole reason that God created us in the first place is so that we can enjoy living in his creation and be thankful to him. But because of sin, our bodies get old and sick. And sometimes, there are accidents and people get hurt so badly that doctors can't help them. Eventually, our bodies will die because of sin.

Before the first sin, man's body was not subject to death and decay. If there was no sin, people could have lived forever. Before the first sin, there was no pain or sickness. The human body was more spiritual than the body we inhabit now. It was not like the body we now have.

By being ever closer to God in love, by seeking God's company rather than physical pleasure, man was to become ever more in the likeness of God. Since God is infinite and beyond any measure, the path of union with God was never to end. That was man's original purpose. But as we all now know and experience every day, sin brought all of creation into a state of corruption and death.

When a person dies, the soul is separated from the body. Body and soul will remain separated until Jesus comes again. At the final judgment, everyone will stand before Jesus as a full person, with body and soul. For this to happen, the body must be resurrected and be united with the soul. This will happen when Jesus comes again, just before the final judgment.

Because of the corruption of the world due to sin, we're going to need incorruptible bodies to enjoy living in the presence of God. Your resurrected body will be a bit different from the way it is now. It won't get sick or broken. It will be spiritual and incorruptible, and you will live forever. But it will still be your body and everyone will still know it's you. The resurrected body will be immortal, living forever.

And those who are still alive when Jesus returns will also be changed - their bodies, like those of the dead, will be made immortal. And each body will have its own individuality. It is a wonderful thing to think about that our new bodies will be identical in form to the glorious body of the resurrected Jesus, no longer suffering the consequence of sin.

There were a lot of witnesses to the bodily resurrection of Jesus Christ. At one point, more than 500 people saw Jesus after he was raised from the dead. The historical fact of the Jesus' resurrection is Heaven's guarantee that we too shall be raised. Jesus is the firstborn of the resurrection which will happen when he comes again.

It is only by power of God the Creator that Jesus was resurrected. And it is only by the power of the resurrected God-Redeemer that all mankind will be resurrected at the Second Coming. Sin brought the corruption of physical death, and the eternal torment of the Second Death, which is the timeout that lasts forever. But it is the resurrection that takes away that sin and the corruption and death that it brings.

God-Redeemer gives us life through His death on the Cross and His Resurrection. To understand what it means to be given life, it is important to understand the death we have been born into. Because of sin, man's nature was changed. Even though we still have the image of God in us, we have become corrupted. This spiritual corruption makes our body subject to decay after death.

We are born into that spiritual corruption with an inherited tendency or inclination toward sin. All of us sin, and so we deserve the consequences of sin which is spiritual and physical death, and eternal timeout from God. So a perfect, blameless sacrifice was needed - a man who is without sin - in order to destroy the consequences of sin. That's why Jesus was born. God-Redeemer came into the world to restore what was lost.

But Jesus did even more than that. He not only restored us, Jesus makes it possible for us to become what people were supposed to be if there had never been sin in the first place. By taking on our sins, as our scapegoat, we are freed from the corruption brought by those sins. Through his death on the cross and through his resurrection, Jesus heals us and gives us life.

When a person dies, their spirit/soul is immediately removed from the constraints of time and space of the 3-dimensional creation. In other words, where the spirit/soul goes is outside of time and so in terms of our 3-dimensional world, they go immediately to the time of the Second Coming and are immediately resurrected with a new spiritual body.

For us still living on Earth, it will seem as if they traveled in Time to whenever the Second Coming actually happens - perhaps 1,000,000 years in the future or more; or less. It's the sort of thing that you see in science fiction shows like "Dr. Who". Only that "void" outside the Universe is not a void at all - it's where God is.

Jesus' resurrection is a declaration of victory over death. With the resurrection of the dead and the final judgment, death is abolished. The end of the world does not mean some sort of catastrophic cataclysm but rather change and finality. Sin will disappear. Everyone will proceed to eternal union with God or to eternal timeout. Along with the resurrection of the dead, Jesus is bringing a new Heaven and a new Earth that will last forever.

The Final Chapter

What happens when we die? When we die, our spirit/soul is immediately removed from the time and space of creation. In other words, where the spirit/soul goes is outside of time and so in terms of our 3-dimensional world, we go immediately to the time of the Second Coming and are immediately resurrected with a new spiritual body.

It will seem as if we traveled in Time to whenever the Second Coming actually happens. It could happen 1,000,000 years in the future or more. It could be less. Only God the Father knows exactly when. It's the sort of thing that you see in science fiction shows like "Dr. Who". Only that "void" outside the Universe is not a void at all - it's where God is.

With the resurrection of the dead and the final judgment, death is abolished. The end of the world does not mean some sort of catastrophic cataclysm but rather change and finality. Sin will disappear from God's Family. Everyone will proceed to eternal union with God or to eternal timeout. When he comes again, Jesus will bring a new Heaven and a new Earth that will last forever.

When someone in God's Family dies, they are no longer separated from God. They are part of God's Family in Heaven. Our Church on Earth is a blurry picture of what that Church in Heaven is like. Some have said the Church on Earth is a shadow of the Church in Heaven. God's Family is one family and that family gathers together in God's One Church.

Those who have died the physical death move from the congregation on Earth to the congregation in Heaven, but they are still part of God's Family. It's like when you go to Mommy's congregation when you're with Mommy, and Daddy's congregation when you're with Daddy. You go to two congregations, but you're still part of God's family whether you go to one or the other.

Heaven will be eternal communion with God which is what God wanted in the beginning of creation. We will be without sin; filled with the Spirit and in full communion with God - but not perfect. Only God is perfect. Jesus is God, so he is perfect. But people are not perfect. We weren't created to be perfect. When God created man, he saw that it was good - not perfect. Our resurrected selves will be as before the first sin.

We were created to be in full communion with God and in a continual process of becoming like God, but not to become God. As we are finite and God is infinite, the process of becoming like Jesus is never-ending - like pouring cereal into a bowl that keeps growing. The transition from the congregation on Earth to the congregation in Heaven is only the beginning - not an ending, just as being baptised into God's Family was just the beginning for you.

In what way are the people in God's Family in Heaven being transformed? The same way as the people in his family on Earth are being transformed: from being self-centered to being "other-centered". It is pride that causes us to turn from God, thinking that we are wiser. So it is pride that must be put in proper perspective. The whole reason that God-Redeemer became a man is to show us how to put away our pride.

How does God's Family in Heaven express such transformation? Pretty much the same way God's Family on Earth expresses it. We are all one big family, after all. God's Family in Heaven is strongly connected with God's Family on Earth. When people in God's Family die, they still remain a vital part of the Church. They are alive in Jesus and "registered in heaven". They worship God and inhabit His heavenly dwelling places.

In taking part in the Eucharist, we come "to the city of the living God" and join in communion with those in God's Family in Heaven in our worship of God, which is why it's also called "Communion". The word eucharist comes from a Greek word meaning "giving thanks". God's Family in Heaven are the saints that are the great "cloud of witnesses" which surrounds us, and we seek to imitate them in "running the race that is set before us". Rejecting or ignoring the communion of saints is a denial that those who have died in Christ are still part of his Holy Church.

Even though God's Family (the saints) lives simultaneously in two dimensions, the heavenly and the earthly, its worship is focused on the heavenly realm. God does not come to us that we might worship him. Rather, we go to him, to His heavenly kingdom, to the heavenly Holy of Holies. This is made clear when the pastor says "Welcome to your Father's House".

Worship begins with an announcement of God's Kingdom which is present here and now. Our ascent into the Heavenly Realm then begins! From an earthly standpoint, we gather for worship in a building with icons, candles, and an altar - all of which are biblical and necessary. But by the power of the Holy Spirit, our worship is conducted in the Heavenly Realm. And present in that worship are God the Father, God the Son, God the Holy Spirit, the holy angels, and the saints enrolled in heaven.

In worship, God's Family on earth joins God's Family in heaven as one family in praise and thanksgiving to God - Father, Son, Holy Spirit. There are numerous witness statements that describe worship in the Heavenly Realm. In one, we see worship in heaven through the eyes of the prophet Isaiah who lived about 700 years before Jesus became man.

Isaiah was caught up into the heavenly dimension and describes what took place. He says, "I saw the Lord sitting on a throne, high and lifted up, and the train of His robe filled the temple." Present as well were the seraphim singing: "Holy, Holy, Holy is the Lord of hosts; The whole earth is full of His glory." Isaiah goes on to describe the building in detail. It is significant that one of the seraphim takes a set of tongs and removes a coal from the altar and with it touches Isaiah's lips, saying, "Behold this has touched your lips, your iniquity is taken away, and your sin is purged."

The connection between Isaiah's vision and the Eucharist (communion) cannot be overlooked! Heavenly worship is real - the ultimate reality. Just as Isaiah experienced the liturgy of heaven, so we, too, joined to Christ and risen with Him in the Heavenly Realm, may enter His presence in heavenly worship.

Another witness statement reminds us that we are surrounded by a great cloud of witnesses. These witnesses are the saints who have gone on before us to their rest, in this case, the "greats" of the times before Jesus became man. This witness statement tells again of our ascent as part of God's Family into the Heavenly Realm. For we have come to the city of the living God, the heavenly Jerusalem. There is an innumerable company of angels. In that city are the general assembly and God's family in heaven - all the spirits of those with God's grace.

God's Family on earth is actually stepping into the heavenly dimension for worship. God himself is present as are the saints and the angels. With something so wondrous it's hard to imagine why any of God's Family would not jump at the chance to experience this encounter with God whenever the church doors are opened.

That's a bit about what Heaven is like. But what does God mean by the Second Death? What does God mean by the Eternal Fire? Hell is a permanent timeout - a permanent spiritual separation from God. Hell will be a dark place just as those who rejected the miracles that Jesus performed right in front of them remained in a darkness of the mind, not filled with light. But that darkness is self-inflicted due to the state of the heart.

Which is where punishment comes in - the unsaved will be punishing themselves due to their own choices. The Light of Jesus is the fiery torment that exists within the heart of the person who is spiritually separated from God, thereby creating a darkness in the mind - much like a clinically depressed person just cannot see the good things in their life because they are overwhelmed with inexplicable despair. There will be weeping and gnashing of teeth.

Think about people like medical doctors who don't have the saving grace of Jesus in their heart; who made their work their "all" instead of God. They will find themselves without purpose at the Second Coming since there won't be anymore sickness. The same goes for lawyers, politicians, accountants, garbage collectors, teachers, etc. Anyone who makes their "all" something other than God will have essentially wasted their entire lives and have nothing to show for it but a burning regret after the Resurrection.

There will be some sort of physical separation between the saved and unsaved because we will all have bodies of some sort and those who can't stand the Light of Jesus will try to get away from it, just as people will try to get away from a burning forest fire. But Satan and his demons won't be in charge in that physical Hell. The gates to Hell are locked from within the heart of those who didn't accept the saving Grace of Jesus.

Because of sin, the world has become polluted and sick. There is constant decay. There is always death. People thoughtlessly waste the things God has provided in this world. In order for God's Family to live forever in God's presence, the world will have to be cleaned up by God. It will have to be a new creation. Maybe it will even be another "Big Bang".

After the Resurrection and removal of sin, good stewardship will be our natural inclination, instead of sin. There won't be rude people selfishly wasting what God has given us. We will take care of the creation, the way God intended for us in the first place. Enjoying the creation and giving thanks to God for it will be the order of the day.

And here we come full circle back to the beginning. God created the Heavens and the Earth in the first place. And this time, with the new Heaven and new Earth, we will be able to not only see the beauty of the creation, we will be able to see the full glory of God-Creator. And it won't be just some of the time, but all of the time, forever and ever. Amen.

Parents' Guide

The idea that I want to get across to every parent and child who reads this book is that what we believe as Christians isn't because of what the Bible says. What we believe as Christians is because that's what God's creation and the Holy Spirit reveal to us about God's Word (**Jn 1:1-4**) - Jesus. The imprint of the Word of God is found all around us, in all of his Creation (**Col 1:15-18**). God spoke and things happened (**Gn 1:1-26**).

In his book <u>Mere Christianity</u>, Lewis starts off using the logic that led him from being an avowed atheist to being a convicted Christian. He talks about the idea of "Natural Law" - what we call "conscience" or our "sense of right and wrong". As Lewis put it, it is because we have a "conscience" that we know that God exists. That conscience is God's law that he has written on our hearts (**Heb 10:16**). Lewis goes on to talk about how the Christ had to be God who became man in order for us to be in communion with God (**Jn 1:12**). Nowhere in the whole book does Lewis cite a single chapter or verse out of the Bible. And I like that approach as there are so many misinterpretations of the Bible out there.

The idea of Biblical Inerrancy is a doctrine that did not come to the Church through the Apostles or even the early Church Fathers. According to the <u>Oxford Companion to the Bible</u>, the term "inerrancy" doesn't even appear in Christian writings before the 1800s. The rigid insistence that each word in the Bible is put there by God himself has led to an unnecessary and embarrassing rejection of science (the Natural

Revelation of God's Word) for hundreds of years.

For instance, in the 1500s, after the voyages of Columbus to the "New World", both John Calvin and Martin Luther rejected the notion that the Earth rotates on its axis and revolves around the sun, going so far as to condemn Copernicus as a heretic deceived by Satan. The mistake of adhering to the doctrine of "literal inerrancy" forced the Presbyterian Church in 1969 to repudiate its previous positions regarding science and theology first elucidated with the conviction of James Woodrow in 1884 as a heretic. Entire generations of Presbyterians were turned against science for over 80 years, and to what end? So the skeptics can easily turn our children who are indoctrinated with the dogma of inerrancy!

The Bible itself does say that all the Holy Scriptures are "God breathed" (**2Tm 3:16**) but you know what else is "God breathed"? You. Me. Every person who has ever been born and has a soul (**Gn 2:7**). When God breathed the spirit of life into man, he saw that it was good - not perfect (**Gn 1:31**). Infallible in the original theological sense means trustworthy - without deceit. And that's what the Bible is - trustworthy and without deceit - but not perfect.

When I was a child, my mother told me to look both ways before crossing the road and stay on the sidewalk instead of walking down the middle of the street. If I didn't look both ways, I might not see oncoming traffic. If I stepped out in front of a car, bad things could happen, like broken bones, maybe even death.

In fact, when I was about 10-years-old, I was walking down the middle of the street by my grandmother's house one day when a VW Beetle turned the corner and hit me. I was knocked off the road onto the grass by the sidewalk. Thankfully the driver was taking a turn and wasn't going that fast. My only injury was to my pride.

My mother isn't perfect. She has a lifetime of experience, but she's not inerrant. And yet, I can still trust her when she tells me that stepping in front of an oncoming car will have negative consequences for my well-being. Inerrancy, or perfection, is not required for conveying truth. As I grew up, my mother and I did not have a very good relationship with each other. No matter how much I wanted her to be perfect, my mother still made mistakes. But that reality doesn't negate all the true things my mother taught me growing up.

I know that my mother still loves me as much as she ever did, and I love her as well. I may have difficulty reconciling the things that happened as a young boy, but my faith tells me that she wants what is best for me despite our issues. While I may find some mistakes in what she has said or done, that doesn't mean she suddenly becomes an untrustworthy liar. She's not perfect, but I can still trust that she says what is true to the best of her ability.

The truth that the Bible conveys does not depend on the writers' perfection. The reality of the Bible is that it was written by flawed people. Maybe you're thinking that the Bible was written by Jesus, the Holy Spirit, God. If that's what you believe, then I advise you to read it again since numerous books of the Bible explicitly state their human authorship - every one of Paul's letters for instance. And on at least one occasion Paul explicitly says that he's expressing his own opinion - **not** God's (**1Cor 7:25**).

God breathed his truth into the hearts and minds of people and the result was that the Bible was created. The people who wrote the Bible weren't perfect. Which is why Paul says "*For now we see in a mirror dimly, but then face to face. Now I know in part; then I shall know fully, even as I have been fully known*" (**1Cor 13:12**). If Paul had believed the Bible was perfect, he could have simply said "We fully know because we have scripture." But he didn't because he knew his source of knowledge is simply God-breathed and is not God himself.

God doesn't make mistakes, but men do (**Ps 18:30**). God is not inconsistent, but men are (**Is 55:8-9**). The Bible is the written testimony of men about God and mankind's relationship with him. As I point out in chapter 3, just because witnesses differ in details doesn't mean that someone is lying. Different people see things differently and so what they see as the truth may also differ. It doesn't make them less trustworthy or deceitful. And that's how it is with the Bible.

Think about what happened at Pentecost after the Christ ascended to heaven: About three thousand souls were converted to the Gospel of Christ (**Ac 2:41**) several decades before even one word of the New Covenant was put to pen and paper. God promised to write his Word on our hearts - not on paper (**Heb 10:16**). And that's what I want to do for my daughter. I tried to follow the example of C.S. Lewis in his approach for <u>Mere Christianity</u> - there's not a single "proof text" from the Bible and yet he makes the case for Christ with such sweet eloquence.

There are two reasons that I don't want to use the Bible as the starting point for teaching my daughter about being Christian. First, I've seen far too many people misuse scripture and turn the Bible into both a hammer and an idol. For me, simply referring to it as "The Word of God" borders on idolatry since we are told, in the Bible itself, that Jesus is the "Word of God" (**Jn 1:1-4**) and the Bible is not Jesus. Second, my daughter is going to run into skeptics that will point out the many contradictions in the Bible, so her faith in God needs to be based on something outside of what the Bible says.

What kind of contradictions is she going to run into? Some stories are told multiple times in the various books of the Bible. One such story that appears twice is found in **2Sm 24:1-25** and again in **1Ch 21:1-30**. David sends Joab and the commanders of the army to take a census of Israel and Judah. There are two big discrepancies between the two versions: 1) One version (**2Sm**) says God incited David to take the census just as he commanded Abraham to sacrifice his son, Isaac. The other version (**1Ch**) says Satan incited him. 2) **2Sm** numbers the men of Israel as 800,000 and the men of Judah as 500,000. **1Ch** numbers the men of Israel as 1,100,000 and the men of Judah as 470,000.

Then there's the question of who killed Goliath. We all know the story where David killed Goliath (**1Sm 17:1-58**). So then why does the Bible say later that Elhanan son of Ariorgim slew Goliath (**2Sm 21:19**)?

How big was the family of Jacob when they went into Egypt? Three places in the Old Testament say 70 (**Gn**

46:27, **Ex 1:5**, **Dt 10:22**). But the first Christian martyr, Stephen, says that there were 75 (**Ac 7:14**). When someone says that Jesus, the Holy Spirit, or God wrote the Bible, the unintended implication is that God is faulty and can't keep his math or facts straight.

That said, the main ideas covered in this book can be found in the Bible. Every chapter covers a part of the Apostles' and Nicene Creeds, except chapter 10, "One Baptism", which is mentioned in just the Nicene Creed. Each section of this Parents' Guide includes the pertinent Bible references along with the applicable portions of the Apostles' and Nicene Creeds.

The version of the Bible I've used for this Guide is the World English Bible because it includes the full canon of Scripture as received by the Apostles and the early Church Fathers. This version is in the Public Domain, and may be reproduced without restriction. It can be downloaded from this website:
https://worldenglish.bible/.
Or, a printed copy may be purchased through this link:
https://ebible.org/buy.php.

As there are no standards for abbreviating the names of the books of the Bible, here are the ones I'm familiar with and use in this Parents' Guide:

Genesis	**Gn**	*Exodus*	**Ex**	*Leviticus*	**Lv**	*Numbers*	**Num**
Deuteronomy	**Dt**	*Joshua*	**Jos**	*Judges*	**Jdg**	*Ruth*	**Ru**
1Samuel	**1Sm**	*2Samuel*	**2Sm**	*1Kings*	**1Kgs**	*2Kings*	**2Kgs**
1Chronicles	**1Ch**	*2Chronicles*	**2Ch**	*1Esdras*	**1Esd**	*Ezra/ Nehemiah (2Esdras)*	**Ezr/ Neh**
Tobit	**Tb**	*Judith*	**Jdt**	*Esther*	**Est**	*1Maccabees*	**1Mc**

2Maccabees	2Mc	3Maccabees	3Mc	4Maccabees	4Mc	Job	Jb
Psalms	Ps	Proverbs	Pr	Ecclesiastes	Ecc	Song of Songs	Sng
Wisdom	Wi	Sirach	Sir	Isaiah	Is	Jeremiah	Jer
Lamentations	Lm	Baruch	Ba	Ltr of Jer.	Ltj	Ezekiel	Ek
Daniel	Dn	Hosea	Hos	Joel	Jl	Amos	Am
Obadiah	Ob	Jonah	Jon	Micah	Mi	Nahum	Na
Habakkuk	Hb	Zephaniah	Zep	Haggai	Hg	Zechariah	Zec
Malachi	Mal	Matthew	Mt	Mark	Mk	Luke	Lk
John	Jn	Acts	Ac	Romans	Rm	1Corinthians	1Co
2Corinthians	2Co	Galatians	Ga	Ephesians	Ep	Philippians	Php
Colossians	Col	1Thessalonian	1Th	2Thessalonian	2Th	1Timothy	1Tm
2Timothy	2Tm	Titus	Ti	Philemon	Phl	Hebrews	Heb
James	Jas	1Peter	1Pt	2Peter	2Pt	1John	1Jn
2John	2Jn	3John	3Jn	Jude	Jd	Revelation	Rv

As I stated in the Introduction, I used the Apostles' Creed as my initial outline, which reads as follows:

Apostles' Creed -

*I believe in God,
the Father almighty,
Creator of heaven and earth,
and in Jesus Christ, his only Son, our Lord,
who was conceived by the Holy Spirit,
born of the Virgin Mary,
suffered under Pontius Pilate,
was crucified, died and was buried;
he descended into hell;
on the third day he rose again from the dead;
he ascended into heaven,
and is seated at the right hand of God the Father almighty;
from there he will come to judge the living and the dead.
I believe in the Holy Spirit,
the holy catholic Church,
the communion of saints,*

the forgiveness of sins,
the resurrection of the body,
and life everlasting. Amen.

The *Apostles' Creed* appears to be based on the old *Roman Creed* known also as the *Old Roman Symbol*, which was itself based on the 2nd-century *Rule of Faith* and the confession of faith for those receiving baptism. The earliest known mention of the expression "Apostles' Creed" occurs in a letter dated 390CE and may have been associated with the belief that each of the Twelve Apostles contributed an article to the twelve articles of the creed.

I also used the Nicene Creed which reads:

Nicene Creed -

I believe in one God,
the Father Almighty,
maker of heaven and earth,
and of all things visible and invisible;
And in one Lord Jesus Christ,
the Only Begotten Son of God,
begotten of his Father before all worlds,
God of God, Light of Light,
very God of very God,
begotten, not made,
being of one substance with the Father;
by whom all things were made;
who for us men and for our salvation
came down from heaven,
and was incarnate by the Holy Ghost of the Virgin Mary,
and was made man;
and was crucified also for us under Pontius Pilate;
he suffered and was buried;
and the third day he rose again according to the Scriptures,
and ascended into heaven,
and sitteth on the right hand of the Father;

and he shall come again, with glory,
to judge both the quick and the dead;
whose kingdom shall have no end.
And I believe in the Holy Ghost the Lord, the Giver of Life,
who proceedeth from the Father;
who with the Father and the Son together is worshiped
and glorified;
who spake by the Prophets.
And I believe one holy Catholic and Apostolic Church;
I acknowledge one Baptism for the remission of sins;
and I look for the resurrection of the dead,
and the life of the world to come. Amen

The *Nicene Creed* is a statement of belief widely used in the Christian Church. It is called Nicene because it was originally adopted in the city of Nicaea by the First Council of Nicaea in 325. In 381, it was amended at the First Council of Constantinople, and the amended form is referred to as the Nicene or the *Niceno-Constantinopolitan Creed*.

Because the earlier Apostles' Creed does not explicitly affirm the divinity of the Son and the Holy Spirit, the Nicene Creed explicitly describes the co-essential divinity of the Son, applying to him the term "consubstantial". It also speaks of the Holy Spirit as worshipped and glorified with the Father and the Son. The Nicene Creed also includes the mention of "one Baptism" because of events which happened after the formation of the Apostles' Creed regarding re-baptism and lapsed Christians.

God the Father, Maker of Everything

Apostles' Creed: *I believe in God, the Father almighty, Creator of heaven and earth,*

Nicene Creed: *I believe in one God, the Father almighty, maker of heaven and earth, of all things visible and invisible.*

Gn 1:1, 2:4, 3:1-24, Ex 31:17, Ps 89:11-13, Sir 42:15-43:33, Is 63:16, Mt 6:9, 23:9, Mk 12:29, 12:32, Lk 4:2-13, 11:2, Ac 4:24, 14:15, 2Cor 6:18, Ep 3:9, 4:6, Col 1:16, Heb 11:3, Rv 4:11

There are two main points that I want to get across in Chapter 1. First, the evidence of God is everywhere and there's no excuse for rejecting him. It is written in the Scriptures:

26 When at the first God created his works
*   and, as he made them, assigned their tasks,*
27 He arranged for all time what they were to do,
*   their domains from generation to generation.*
They were not to go hungry or grow weary,
*   or ever cease from their tasks.*
28 Never does a single one crowd its neighbor,
*   or do any ever disobey his word.*
29 Then the Lord looked upon the earth,
*   and filled it with his blessings.*
30 Its surface he covered with every kind of living creature
*   which must return into it again* (**Sir 16:26-30**).

Second, the reason we can't see God himself is because of sin (**Rm 1:20-21**). Satan used temptation (**Gn 3:1-5**) to twist man's freewill,

"God in the beginning created human beings
*   and made them subject to their own free choice"* (**Sir 15:14**).

and now God wishes for our return to him:

24 But to the penitent he provides a way back
*   and encourages those who are losing hope!*
25 Turn back to the Lord and give up your sins,
*   pray before him and make your offenses few.*
26 Turn again to the Most High and away from iniquity,
*   and hate intensely what he loathes.* (**Sir 17:24-26**).

While science can't prove or disprove the existence of God, it can show us something of how God does things, how he uses both chaos and order.

The difficult concept to explain is why Satan brings temptation. What is he trying to prove? The answer lies in the beginning of **Job** (**Jb 1:6-2:9**). What Satan is trying to show God is that mankind only worships him and praises him because we don't want to end up in Eternal Damnation, that we only love him when we feel blessed. Satan seems to believe that we aren't worthy of God, or to be in communion with him. God disagrees:

*11 That is why the Lord is patient with them
   and pours out his mercy on them.
12 He sees and understands that their death is wretched,
   and so he forgives them all the more.
13 Their compassion is for their neighbor,
   but the Lord's compassion reaches all flesh,
   Reproving, admonishing, teaching,
   and turning them back, as a shepherd his flock.
14 He has compassion on those who accept his discipline,
   who are eager for his precepts.* (**Sir 18:11-14**).

Something that I didn't go into with my daughter, but is important for any parent to think about is perhaps the most common objection by skeptics regarding God. In my many discussions with skeptics about God, inevitably they will pull out what they view as their trump card which goes something like this: *If there is an almighty God, why do bad things happen?* They'll talk about mass murderers, genocide, serial killers, child molesters and kids dying from cancer.

It is crucial for the young Christian to know that sometimes bad things do happen to you even when you believe in God, Jesus and the Holy Spirit - even when you pray every day. It might be tempting to point out that the entire book of Job addresses this very issue, but it doesn't really answer it. After Job whines and complains about all the undeserved bad things that happened ("*Why me, O God?*") God never really answers him. God simply responds by saying "*Who are you to question me, the Creator of the Universe?*" But other shorter passages do tell us that sometimes bad things do happen even to good people:

*1 The wisdom of the poor lifts their head high
  and sets them among princes.
2 Do not praise anyone for good looks;
  or despise anyone because of appearance.
3 The bee is least among winged creatures,
  but it reaps the choicest of harvests.
4 Do not mock the one who wears only a loin-cloth,
  or scoff at a person's bitter day.
For strange are the deeds of the Lord,
  hidden from mortals his work.* (**Sir 11:1-4**)

Jesus Christ, Only Son of God

Apostles' Creed: *I believe in Jesus Christ, his only Son, our Lord.*

Nicene Creed: *I believe in one Lord Jesus Christ, the Only Begotten Son of God, born of the Father before all ages. God from God, Light from Light, true God from true God, begotten, not made, one substance with the Father; through him all things were made;*

Ps 2:7, Wi 7:26, 18:14-25, Jn 1:1-4, 1:9-10, 1:14, 1:18, 3:16, 16:28, Ac 13:33, Rm 11:36, 1Cor 3:24, 8:6, 2Cor 4:6, Ep 4:5, Col 1:15-17, 2:9, Heb 1:3, 1:10, 5:5, 1Jn 1:5, 4:9, 5:20

There's an old saying that "hindsight is 20/20." Basically, things always seem clearer after the fact. In sports, armchair quarterbacks incessantly talk about what should have happened when the actual players on the field make what they deem a "bad" play. Doctors are frequently sued for medical procedures that don't go the way patients and their families expect. Along those same lines, many Christians say with the same confidence of Peter (**Lk 22:33**) that if they had lived back then, they'd have recognized Jesus as God.

But would they? Consider that Satan and all the angelic host were in the very presence of God, and yet a full 1/3 fell away and turned from God (**Rv 12:4**). How many Christians will follow the example of Tobias and his father in the face of adversity?

3 Tobiah went out to look for some poor person among our kindred, but he came back and cried, "Father!" I said to him, "Here I am, son." He answered, "Father, one of our people has been murdered! He has been thrown out into the market place, and there he lies strangled." 4 I sprang to my feet, leaving the dinner untouched, carried the dead man from the square, and put him in one of the rooms until sundown, so that I might bury him. 5 I returned and washed and in sorrow ate my food. 6 I remembered the oracle pronounced by the prophet Amos against Bethel: "I will turn your feasts into mourning, and all your songs into dirges." 7 Then I wept. At sunset I went out, dug a grave, and buried him. 8 My neighbors mocked me, saying: "Does he have no fear? Once before he was hunted, to be executed for this sort of deed, and he ran away; yet here he is again burying the dead!" (**Tb 2:3-8**)

How many will follow Peter's example when he feared for his own life (**Lk 22:54-60**)?

Jesus himself tells us that he has much more for us to learn, and that it is the Holy Spirit that will reveal it (**Jn 14:26**) - not just when we're baptised, not just when we

become Christian, but today and all the days of our life -
"Trust in God, and he will help you; make your ways straight and hope in him." (**Sir 2:6**).

Scriptures tell us that it is by God that our eyes are opened to see:
6 Discernment, tongues, and eyes,
*   ears, and a mind for thinking he gave them.*
7 With knowledge and understanding he filled them;
*   good and evil he showed them.* (**Sir 17:6-7**).
In truth, it is by God that we know anything at all
5 Was not the water sweetened by a twig,
*   so that all might learn his power?*
6 He endows people with knowledge,
*   to glory in his mighty works,*
7 through which the doctor eases pain,
8   and the druggist prepares his medicines.
Thus God's work continues without cease
*   in its efficacy on the surface of the earth.* (**Sir 38:5-8**).

The fact remains that only God can bring forgiveness of sin (**Mic 7:18**). That's how we know that the Messiah is in fact God, because as we read in Isaiah he brings that very forgiveness - that healing:
Therefore I will divide him a portion with the many,
*   and he shall divide the spoil with the strong,*
because he poured out his soul to death
*   and was numbered with the transgressors;*
yet he bore the sin of many,
*   and makes intercession for the transgressors.* (**Is 53:12**)

Conceived by the Spirit, Born man

Apostles' Creed: *Who was conceived by the Holy Spirit, born of the Virgin Mary.*

Nicene Creed: *For us men and for our salvation he came down from heaven, and by the Holy Spirit was incarnate of the Virgin Mary, and became man.*

Sir 1:1, Is 7:14, Mt 1:20-23, Lk 1:30-35, Jn 1:14, 3:13, 3:31, 6:38, Gal 4:4, Col 1:13-14, 1Th 5:9, Heb 2:14, 1Jn 4:2

Such nonsense! Why would the Lord God, creator of the universe, lower himself into a tiny, fragile shell as a man? Such a thought made no sense to the Jews. Oh sure, they knew that the "messiah" was coming from the lineage of David, but they expected that the anointed of God would simply be a man, like any other king. That's why they were taken off-guard when Jesus asked why David wrote *"The Lord said to my lord..."* (**Ps 110:1**). It showed that the chosen of God was both man *and* God.

When you think about it though, this makes perfect sense. God's ways are not our ways; God's wisdom is not our wisdom (**Is 55:8-9**). So how then can we possibly hope to understand what God wants for us? God's language does not translate well into any man-made language. The perfect ideas breathed from God into the imperfect minds of humanity will always end up distorted. The Scriptures make this point very clear:

6 No one can lessen, increase,
*   or fathom the wonders of the Lord.*
7 When mortals finish, they are only beginning,
*   and when they stop they are still bewildered.* (**Sir 18:6-7**).

Nobody can duplicate the sounds of God's language which has no vowels or consonants that human beings can articulate. God's very Word is so complex that he had to become incarnate as a whole person instead of being made as sounds on the wind. Jesus became man to show us the way that we might begin to understand and follow God, for we read in the Scriptures:

*17 For he gave me sound knowledge of what exists,
    that I might know the structure of the universe and the
    force of its elements,
18 The beginning and the end and the midpoint of times,
    the changes in the sun's course and the variations of the
        seasons,
19 Cycles of years, positions of stars,
20 natures of living things, tempers of beasts,
    Powers of the winds and thoughts of human beings,
    uses of plants and virtues of roots—
21 Whatever is hidden or plain I learned,
22 for Wisdom, the artisan of all, taught me.* (**Wi 7:17-22**).

I recently had an experience that illustrated to me why God had to become man. Recently, there has been a stray cat that's been hanging around the backyard where there's a storm drain that I can't easily get to. We'd hear him (I think it's a he) meow plaintively - the same way I've had other cats ask to be fed.

This cat is a beautiful orange tiger-stripe, but he's also very wary of people. He won't come close enough for me to touch him, even when I'm offering food. It's nigh impossible for me to let the cat know that I want to help take care of him. And even if I were to become a cat, I'm not sure he'd take to me even then as cats are very territorial - just like people. So then, through my experience with that cat, I have a better understanding of why God became man - so that we could relate to him better.

Suffered, Crucified, Died and Buried

Apostles' Creed: *Suffered under Pontius Pilate, was crucified, died, and was buried.*

Nicene Creed: *For our sake he was crucified under*

Pontius Pilate, he suffered death and was buried,

Wi 2:12-22, Is 53:4-5, Mt 27:50, 27:59-60, Mk 15:15, Jn 19:18, Ac 4:10, 4:27, 1Tm 6:13, 1Pt 2:24

Even more nonsense! The Messiah was supposed to be a conquering king - at least that's what the Jews of Jesus' day expected. Paul even tells us that dying on the cross was complete foolishness (**1Cor 1:18**). But that's how we know the story of Jesus' crucifixion isn't made up. If the Apostles were going to make up a story of a redeeming Messiah, they would have skipped the dying on the cross part of the story. It was completely and utterly shameful and dishonorable to die a criminal's death.

And yet the Jewish leaders should have expected it. It was predicted in their very Scriptures. When Jesus was on the cross, he even quoted the scripture that predicted his death in that manner. He said, "*My God, My God, Why have you forsaken me?*" (**Mt 27:46**). Because of these words from Jesus, some say that part of the agony that Jesus was suffering was being separated from God the Father. I don't agree. Our God is One - one substance and indivisible.

What else could Jesus have meant? Back in those days, there were no chapters and verses in Scripture. When a teacher wanted to refer to scripture, he quoted the first line of the passage. And those words, "*My God, My God ...*" come from **Ps 22:1-31**. The Jewish leaders mocking Jesus at the cross would have recognized it instantly. Jesus was further convicting them in their stiff-necked rejection of him.

The Wisdom Literature of the Old Testament has many, many references to the Executed Messiah. For instance, **Sirach** closes by talking about how the Messiah is put to death, yet rescued by God the Father. I especially like the part which says:

My soul drew near to death,
and my life was on the brink of Hades below.
They surrounded me on every side,
and there was no one to help me;
I looked for human assistance,
and there was none.
Then I remembered your mercy, O Lord,
and your kindness from of old,
for you rescue those who wait for you
and save them from the hand of their enemies. (**Sir 51:6-8**)

Descended to Hell, Rose from Dead

Apostles' Creed: *He descended to hell. On the third day he rose again.*

Nicene Creed: *and rose again on the third day in accordance with the Scriptures.*

Ps 16:10, 102:20, 107:10,13-14,16,20, Sir 24:5, Is 24:21-22, Zec 9:11, Mt 27:40, 67, Mk 8:31, 9:31, 10:36, 16:9, Lk 24:45-46, Jn 20:19-20, 25-29, Ac 2:24,27, 2:31-32, 3:15, 4:33, 10:40, 13:33-37, 1Cor 15:3-4,15:12-22, Ga 1:1, Ep 4:8-10, 1Pt 3:18-20

So what was the Christ up to between the time he breathed his last breath on the cross and when he walked out of the tomb? In **Acts**, the Christ's Descent into Hades is explained quite clearly, "*God raised him up, loosing the pangs of death, because it was not possible for him to be held by it... For you will not abandon my soul to Hades, or let your Holy One see corruption... he foresaw and spoke about the resurrection* *of the Christ, that he was not abandoned to Hades, nor did his flesh see corruption."* (**Ac 2:24,27,31**). In **Ephesians**, we read *"Now this, He ascended, what is it but that he also first descended into the lower parts of the earth?"* (**Eph 4:9**)

While the teaching about the Messiah's descent into Sheol (or, to use the Greek terms: the Christ's descent into Hades), the place of the dead, is not a prominent feature in most Sunday Schools, it is clearly mentioned in several places in the Holy Scriptures. For instance, **1Peter** says

For Christ also suffered once for sins, the righteous for the unrighteous, that he might bring us to God, being put to death in the flesh but made alive in the spirit, in which he went and proclaimed to the spirits in prison, because they formerly did not obey, when God's patience waited in the days of Noah, while the ark was being prepared, in which a few, that is, eight persons, were brought safely through water (**1Pt 3:18-20**).

This event is prophesied in the Old Testament as found in a selection of verses from the **Psalms**, related to the Resurrection of the Christ:

Some sat in darkness, in utter darkness,
*   prisoners suffering in iron chains...*
Then they cried to the Lord in their trouble,
*   and he saved them from their distress.*
He brought them out of darkness, the utter darkness,
*   and broke away their chains...*
for he breaks down gates of bronze
*   and cuts through bars of iron...*
He sent out his word and healed them;
*   he rescued them from the grave.* (**Ps 107:10,13-14,16,20**)

In **Isaiah** and **Zechariah**, it is written

"And God shall bring his hand upon the host of heaven, and upon the kings of the earth. And they shall gather the multitude thereof into prisons, and they shall shut them into a strong hold: after many generations they shall be visited." (**Is 24:21-22**)

and again

"And you by the blood of your covenant has sent forth your prisoners out of the pit that has no water." (**Zec 9:11**)

In **Job,** God speaks to Job out of a whirlwind and asks him *"Where were you when I founded the earth? Tell me now, if you have knowledge, who set the measures of it, if you know? Or who stretched a line upon it? ... Or did I order the morning light in your time? ... Or did you take clay of the ground, and form a living creature, and set it with the power of speech upon the earth? ... And do the gates of death open to you for fear; and did the porters of hell quake when they saw you?"* (**Jb 38:4-17** Septuagint)

This last portion from the Book of Job in the Septuagint is quite different from the Masoretic Text. In the New Revised Standard Version (NRSV) it reads as follows: *"Have the gates of death been revealed to you, or have you seen the gates of deep darkness?"* Very different and not much in the way of prophecy of the Christ's Descent to the Dead. As a prophecy, it has all the punch and impact of wilted lettuce.

Finally, as I said before, **Sirach** closes with that same prophecy of crucifixion and victory over the Grave, saying,
"You have been my helper and delivered me ... from choking fire on every side, and from the midst of fire that I had not kindled, from the deep belly of Hades... My soul drew near to death, and my life was on the brink of Hades below. They surrounded me on every side, and there was no one to help me; I looked for human assistance, and there was none. Then I remembered your mercy, O Lord ... for you rescue those who wait for you and save them from the hand of their enemies." (**Sir 51:2-8**)

Clearly, the Descent to the Grave is a vital work of the Christ's Ministry on Earth. The implications of that event in the Christ's work of salvation can't be over-emphasized. It was important enough that the Holy Spirit remained with Jesus as he declared victory over

death, for Scripture tells us
13 When a righteous man was sold,
wisdom didn't forsake him,
but she delivered him from sin.
She went down with him into a dungeon,
14 and in bonds she didn't depart from him,
until she brought him the sceptre of a kingdom,
and authority over those that dealt like a tyrant with him.
She also showed those who had mockingly accused him to be false,
and gave him eternal glory (**Wi 10:13-14**).

Ascended to Heaven

Apostles' Creed: *He ascended into heaven and sits at the right hand of God the Father Almighty.*

Nicene Creed: *He ascended into heaven and is seated at the right hand of the Father*

Ps 110:1, Mk 16:19, Lk 22:69, 24:51, Jn 14:16-17, 16:5-7, 17:5, Ac 1:9-11, 2:33, 5:31, 7:55-56, Ep 4:8-10, Heb 4:14, 8:1, 9:24, 12:2, 1Pt 3:21-22

Just as the Descent into Hades is a vital part of the Christ's work, so is his ascension. When Jesus, God-Redeemer, declared victory over death, God-Creator glorifies the Son in Heaven. The Scriptures tell us:
3 They shall say among themselves,
rueful and groaning through anguish of spirit:
This is the one whom once we held as a laughingstock
*   and as a type for mockery,*
4 fools that we were!
His life we accounted madness,
*   and death dishonored.*
5 See how he is accounted among the heavenly beings;
*   how his lot is with the holy ones!* (**Wi 5:3-5**)

This ascension demonstrates Christ's glorification. Jesus' work on Earth was done. According to Mark, "*After the Lord Jesus had spoken to them, he was taken up into heaven and he sat at the right hand of God*" (**Mk 16:19**). He left earth in his physical form going into his former place of glory, being victorious over death (**Jn 17:5**) and fulfilling the Scriptures:

The Lord says to my lord:
  "Sit at my right hand,
  while I make your enemies your footstool" (**Ps 110:1**).

Jesus' ascension began the time of his ministry as God in the Church. God ministers through his Word and his prophets in the Church. Christ's body on the earth is now the Church (**Eph 5:30, 4:15-16**). The ascension is the bridge between all that Jesus began to do and to teach (**Ac 1:1**), and what the apostles and the church continued to do and to teach afterward. The Scriptures foretold that the Christ Jesus would "*Give new signs and work new wonders; show forth the splendor of your right hand and arm*" (**Sir 36:6-7**).

God the Father sent the Holy Spirit to dwell in believers, taking the place of Jesus' bodily presence, and continuing his earthly ministry (**Jn 14:16-17; 16:5-7**). *All this I have spoken while still with you. But the Counselor, the Holy Spirit, whom the Father will send in my name, will teach you all things and will remind you of everything I have said to you* (**Jn 14:25-26**).
And,
He will bring glory to me by taking from what is mine and making it known to you (**Jn 16:14**).

By the power of the Spirit, Jesus lives in believers and continues his work in and through them. It is just as the Scriptures foretold:

*⁵ The vault of heaven I compassed alone,
  and walked through the deep abyss.*
*⁶ Over waves of the sea, over all the land,
  over every people and nation I held sway.*
*⁷ Among all these I sought a resting place.
  In whose inheritance should I abide?* (**Sir 24:5-7**)

This man, Jesus - appointed as sin by God-Creator - is our scapegoat (**2Co 5:21**). He was humiliated and shamed on our behalf. But then God-Creator did the unthinkable! The Psalmist writes:

*²⁸ All the ends of the earth
    will remember and turn to the Lord;
  All the families of nations
    will bow low before him.*
*²⁹ For kingship belongs to the Lord,
    the ruler over the nations* (**Ps 22:28-29**).

The ascension is the assurance of his return. He said: *And if I go and prepare a place for you, I will come back and take you to be with me that you also may be where I am* (**Jn 14:3**).

Jesus Will Come Again in Glory

Apostles' Creed: *Whence He shall come to judge the living and the dead.*

Nicene Creed: *He will come again in glory to judge the living and the dead and his kingdom will have no end.*

Mt 16:27, Mk 13:26, Jn 5:22-23, 14:3, Ac 10:42, Rm 14:10, 2Cor 5:10, 1Th 4:17, 2Tm 4:1, Heb 1:8, 1Pt 4:4-5, 2Pt 1:11

Scripture is very clear about what will happen when Jesus returns in Glory. Those who truly accept his New Covenant will be vindicated, as it is written:
11 For the Lord is full of compassion and mercy,

long suffering, and very pitiful,
and forgives sins,
and saves in time of affliction.
12 Woe be to fearful hearts, and faint hands,
and the sinner that goes two ways!
13 Woe to him that is fainthearted! for he believes not;
therefore shall he not be defended.
14 Woe to you that have lost patience!
and what will you do when the Lord shall visit you?
15 They that fear the Lord will not disobey his Word;
and they that love him will keep his ways.
16 They that fear the Lord will seek that which is well, pleasing to
him;
and they that love him shall be filled with the law.
17 They that fear the Lord will prepare their hearts,
and humble their souls in his sight,
18 Saying, We will fall into the hands of the Lord,
and not into the hands of men:
for as his majesty is, so is his mercy. (**Sir 2:11-18**)

What are we supposed to do while waiting for Jesus to return? Scripture tells us *"Work at your tasks in due season, and in his own time God will give you your reward"* (**Sir 51:30**). There have been quite a few people who have claimed that they knew exactly when Jesus would return. And they were all wrong. They are false prophets and teachers.

The fact is that Jesus himself said that only the Father knows when Jesus will return. Not the angels, not the Son or the Holy Spirit (**Mt 24:36**). Jesus said the point of God the Father keeping such knowledge to only himself is to keep us on our toes. God doesn't want us to wait to the last minute to accept the Gospel of Salvation.

However, Satan is still out in the world, deceiving many people. There have been some of those who have falsely claimed to be sent by God. And until Jesus comes again,

there will always be more such people (**1Jn 2:18-23**). But how do we know that such people are not sent by God? Because Jesus promised us two things:
1. He himself would come back in glory and *nobody* would miss it (**Mt 24:30**); and
2. The person sent by God is the Holy Spirit who is invisible without a physical body (**Jn 14:26**).

Now what about all the bad things we hear about on the news: hurricanes, tornadoes, earthquakes, climate change, wars? Don't those things mean Jesus is coming really soon? No. Jesus even told us that those sort of things were only the beginning of the troubles that would happen until he comes back from Heaven (**Mt 24:6-8**). There has been and will continue to be great trouble in the world like wars and natural disasters.

Jesus did tell us that he will return after the Good News about his story has been told to every country around the world (**Mt 24:14**). The Holy Spirit will have completed his mission and every living person on Earth will have had a chance to hear the story of Jesus.

The Christ will gather everyone together who accepted him into their heart and followed his example. Scripture tells us, *"Those who serve God to please him are accepted; their petition reaches the clouds"* (**Sir 35:20**). As for the people who rejected the healing salvation of Jesus, they will eternally regret that rejection as they will be knowingly separated from God even as today they are unknowingly isolated. For it is written, *"Later he will rise up and repay them, requiting each one as they deserve"* (**Sir 17:23**).

The Holy Spirit, Giver of Life

Apostles' Creed: *I believe in the Holy Spirit,*

Nicene Creed: *I believe in the Holy Spirit, the Lord, the giver of life, who proceeds from the Father and the Son, who with the Father and the Son is adored and glorified, who has spoken through the prophets*

Ek 39:29, Jn 6:63, 14:26, 15:26, 16:7, Ac 1:8, 2:17, 13:2, 1Cor 2:10-11, 12:13, 2Cor 3:6, 3:8, Ep 3:5, Heb 3:7-9, 1Pt 1:10-11

Who is the the Holy Spirit? We know God-Creator, or God the Father, is the first person of God. We also know that God-Redeemer or God the Son is the second person of God. So when we consider what we know about the Holy Spirit, we know that she is the third person of God. The Holy Spirit is God just as Jesus is God. But the Holy Spirit is not the same person as Jesus or the Father. Scripture has this to say about the Holy Spirit:

6 To whom has the root of wisdom been revealed?
*   or who has known her wise counsels?*
7 To whom has the knowledge of wisdom been made manifest?
*   and who has understood her great experience?*
8 There is one wise and greatly to be feared,
*   the Lord sitting upon his throne.*
9 He created her, and saw her, and numbered her,
*   and poured her out upon all his works.*
10 She is with all flesh according to his gift,
*   and he has given her to them that love him.* (**Sir 1:6-10**)

The empowering presence of the Holy Spirit is everywhere around the world all at once. The Holy Spirit is with me as I write these words while at the same time the Spirit is with you as you read them. And that's what God has desired all along: to reach out to all of mankind, healing everyone's soul, overcoming the separation of sin from God.

24 For wisdom is more moving than any motion:
she passes and goes through all things by reason of her
pureness.
25 For she is the breath of the power of God,
and a pure influence flowing from the glory of the Almighty:
therefore can no defiled thing fall into her
26 For she is the brightness of the everlasting light,
the unspotted mirror of the power of God,
and the image of his goodness.
27 And being but one, she can do all things:
and remaining in herself, she makes all things new:
and in all ages entering into holy souls,
she makes them friends of God, and prophets.
28 For God loves none but him that dwells with wisdom.
29 For she is more beautiful than the sun,
and above all the order of stars:
being compared with the light, she is found before it.
30 For after this comes night:
but vice shall not prevail against wisdom (**Wi 7:24-30**)

The Scriptures tell us that the Holy Ghost is a quiet voice that we hear with our minds, not our ears. But to hear it, sometimes we need to be quiet and willing to listen. Other times, it's like we can't hear or think about anything else but the one thought that Holy Spirit puts into our head (**1Kg 19:11-13**).

The Holy Spirit is co-eternal with the Father and the Son which means that she also exists outside of time and space. It also means that God-Creator didn't create or make God the Spirit like he created mankind. The Spirit has always been with the Father and the Son. Even at the moment of creation, the Holy Spirit was there with the Holy Creator and the Holy Word (**Gn 1:2**). It is only because the Spirit is God that she is able to guide us into communion with the Creator and Redeemer.

Since the Holy Spirit is God just as the Son and the Father are also the one true God, we are expected to worship her. Jesus described the Spirit as a "comforter" (**Jn 14:26**). That is, the Spirit is God who gives us hugs when we need it. And for that, we should give thanks and praise to God the Spirit.

When the Holy Spirit breathes God's Word into our hearts and minds guiding us, that is communicating with us directly. When the Holy Spirit reveals God's Word to us through the world around us or through other people, that is indirect communication. One way the Holy Spirit speaks to us indirectly is through people called prophets. Simply put, a prophet is a spokesperson for God, expounding on what the Creator or Redeemer, through the Holy Spirit, has told them to say (**2Pt 1:21**).

However, there have also been, and always will be, some false prophets who claim mistakenly that their message comes from the Holy Spirit when it didn't (**Mt 24:24, 2Pt 2:1-3**). The way to tell is if the message is untrue at all. If it's not 100% true, then the message is not from God. If a prophet makes a prediction of the future that doesn't come true, then it's not from God. Don't listen to that person about anything (**Dt 18:22**).

Think about listening to recorded music on the radio being played more than once. The singer only sang the song one time, but because of how recordings work, we can hear it over and over. That's how the Holy Spirit brings the redemption of Jesus' death to everyone in the world. Jesus died only once, but by the power of God the Spirit, that death is brought into all people, so that

God's grace washes over everyone. As the Scriptures tell us,

*24 Faint not to be strong in the Lord; that he may confirm
    you, cleave to him:
  for the Lord Almighty is God alone, and beside him there
    is no other Saviour.
25 He fills all things with his wisdom,
    as Phison and as Tigris in the time of the new fruits.
26 He makes the understanding to abound like Euphrates,
    and as Jordan in the time of the harvest.
27 He makes the doctrine of knowledge appear as the light,
    and as Geon in the time of vintage.
28 The first man knew her not perfectly:
    no more shall the last find her out.
29 For her thoughts are more than the sea,
    and her counsels profounder than the great deep.
30 I also came out as a brook from a river,
    and as a conduit into a garden.
31 I said, I will water my best garden, and will water
    abundantly my garden bed:
  and, behold, my brook became a river, and my river
    became a sea.
32 I will yet make doctrine to shine as the morning,
    and will send forth her light afar off.
33 I will yet pour out doctrine as prophecy,
    and leave it to all ages for ever.* (**Sir 24:23-33**)

There is no way for us to accept the sacrifice of Jesus except the Holy Spirit shows us. As the Holy Spirit works through all people, she is nudging them to hear what Jesus, God-Redeemer, has done for them. Our conscience, the sense of right and wrong which everyone has, comes from the Holy Spirit. This sense of Fair Play - of doing the right thing - is how we know God exists at all.

It is through the Holy Spirit that God writes his Word on our heart. Why? When Jesus went back to Heaven, there was so much more that he wanted us to know, but we weren't ready (**Jn 14:26**). So now the Holy Spirit who is inside us teaches us what the Father and the Son want us to know. She doesn't always teach us with a loud voice like thunder but often with a quiet voice like the fluttering of butterfly wings.

We are led to follow Jesus only by the Holy Spirit. That happens because Holy Spirit is in us *before* we accept the Christ as saviour. The Spirit works through both the saved and the unsaved, just as the rain falls on the undeserving as well as the deserving (**Mt 5:45**). That doesn't mean that everyone is saved, however. But in order for those who are not saved to reject the Holy Spirit (the only unforgivable sin) then the Holy Spirit has to be present to be rejected.

Blasphemy against God the Father, our Creator, is a sin. Blasphemy against God the Son, our Redeemer, is also a sin. But those sins will be forgiven if we ask God. But when we blaspheme the Holy Spirit, by rejecting her, that sin won't be forgiven (**Lk 12:10**). It is the only unforgivable sin. How do you know if you've blasphemed the Holy Spirit? If you're asking the question, then you haven't rejected her. It's the people who've truly seared their hearts against the Holy Spirit that won't care and won't ask.

One Church, Communion of Saints

Apostles' Creed: *The holy catholic Church, The communion of saints,*

Nicene Creed: *I believe in one, holy, catholic and apostolic Church.*

Mt 16:18, 28:19, Ac 1:8, 2:42, 9:31, Rm 12:4-13, 15:26-27, 1Co 1:1-2, 1:9, 10:17, 2Co 1:1, 8:3-4, Ep 1:4, 2:20, 4:4, 5:27, Php 2:1-4, 1Tm 3:15, Heb 12:22-25, 1Pt 1:1, 1Jn 1:3

When Christians depart this life, they remain a vital part of the Church, the Body of Christ. They are alive in the Lord and "registered in heaven" (**Heb 12:23**). They worship God (**Rv 4:10**) and inhabit His heavenly dwelling places (**Jn 14:2**). In the Eucharist - the Holy Communion - we come "to the city of the living God" and join in communion with those departed Christians in our worship of God (**Heb 12:22**).

They are that great "cloud of witnesses" which surrounds us, and we seek to imitate them in running "the race that is set before us" (**Heb 12:1**). Rejecting or ignoring this communion of saints is a denial that those who have died in Christ are still part of his Holy Church. Scripture assures us that those who have departed still participate in the same worship as those of us still in the earthly realm:

*For in secret the holy children of the good were offering
   sacrifice
   and carried out with one mind the divine institution,
So that your holy ones should share alike the same blessings
   and dangers,
   once they had sung the ancestral hymns of praise*
(**Wi 18:9**).

God's family includes the prophets and saints of both the Old and New Covenants, the angels and the community of believers in this earthly life. We call those who have died in Christ before us the Church Triumphant, while those still living in this life are called the Church Militant (**Rv 7:9-17**). When a person dies, their spirit/soul is immediately removed from the constraints of time and space of the 3-dimensional creation. In other words, where the spirit/soul goes is outside of time and they go immediately to the time of the Second Coming and are immediately resurrected with a new spiritual body.

For us still living in the earthly realm, it seems as if they traveled in Time to whenever the Second Coming actually happens - perhaps 1,000,000 years in the future or more - or less. To put it in more personal terms, this means that any of our friends and family who have passed on with the saving grace of Jesus has been resurrected and are part of that Church Triumphant. As Jesus told the thief on the cross, *"Today you will be with me in paradise"* (**Lk 23:43**).

The Scriptures tell us quite a bit about the Church Triumphant. We know that the dead in Christ are alive (**Jn 11:25**). Not only are they alive, the dead in Christ are with him (**Jn 14:3**). We also know that nothing separates the dead in Christ from him (**Rm 8:38-39**). It follows then that the dead in Christ are in the heavenly Jerusalem - the City of God (**Heb 12:22-23**).

We are told that "The Elders" - the leadership of the New Israel - are in the very presence of Christ and the Holy Throne (**Rv 5:11**). The Apocalypse of John also shows us that, as part of the transforming process, the Triumphant Brethren offer prayers and thanksgiving just as the Militant Brethren do (**Rv 5:8, 8:3**).

Our resurrected selves will be as Adam was before the fall. Adam was created to be in full communion with God and in a continual process of becoming like God, but not to become God - to say otherwise is to say that the Mormons have it correct. As we are finite and God is infinite, the process of becoming like Jesus is never-ending. The transition from Church Militant to Church Triumphant is only the beginning - not an ending.

So then, upon receiving the resurrected spiritual body, the brethren that are part of the Church Triumphant (which is one Church with the Church Militant) are in the same physical state as Adam prior to the first sin (**Php 3:20-21**).

It is a sinless state in perpetual union with God - not perfect, but without blemish and without sin - as it was intended in the first place. The brethren in the Church Triumphant will spend everlasting life becoming more like God. Since God is infinite, our transformation will be a never-ending one.

If Adam had been perfect before the fall, he would have been infallible. If he had been infallible, then he wouldn't have sinned in the first place. To be perfect is to be God! And that is the sense of pride that brought the fall in the first place. **Mt 5:48** isn't setting a requirement, it's giving us a goal to shoot for.

To use a sports analogy, as Paul did (**1Co 9:24**), it's like athletes competing in diving or gymnastics. The goal is a perfect 10, but that's rarely achieved. I am very reluctant to describe it as "perfection" because that is too close to blasphemy for my comfort.

We will be like Adam before the fall. Without sin - filled with the Spirit - in full communion with God - but not perfect. Only God is perfect. Jesus is God, so he is perfect. But Adam is not perfect. He wasn't created as perfect. When God created man, he saw that it was good - not perfect (**Gn 1:31**).

So then, in what way is the Church Triumphant being transformed? The same way as the Church Militant are being transformed: from being self-centered to being "other-centered". That's the whole point of **Mt 25:31-46** and **Ek 16:49-50**. How is the transformation of the Church Triumphant demonstrated? Through the common worship and prayer alongside the Church Militant.

There's an old saying that two heads are better than one. That means it is easier for two people who help each other to solve a problem than it is for one person to solve a problem alone. It is easier for one person to go "off-track" than it is for many people, just as it's harder to break a rope of many strands than it is to break just one strand. Besides that, being lonely is a very sad feeling. People aren't meant to be alone (**Gn 2:18**). It is for that reason that God created the idea of "family". And that is exactly what the Scriptures tell us about God's family, the Church:

2 Who will apply the lash to my thoughts,
*   and to my mind the rod of discipline,*
That my failings may not be spared
*   or the sins of my heart overlooked?*
3 Otherwise my failings may increase,
*   and my sins be multiplied;*
And I fall before my adversaries,
*   and my enemy rejoice over me?* (**Sir 23:2-3**)

In the congregations of the Church, we learn more about God, have the chance to worship him with other followers of Jesus, and are better able to find ways to serve God by helping others. Church is the place where rejoicing and giving thanks to God becomes easy (**Heb 10:24-25**). The many congregations, which are also called churches, are still one big family: one body with many parts (**1Cor 12:12-27**). And even though congregations may differ from each other in the way they worship and praise God, they are still part of the same family of God.

In these modern times, the main reason that people become members of a particular congregation is to gather together for prayer and worship of God in a way that touches their heart. While different congregations of the true Church may have different ways to worship God, they all have a few things in common.

Every gathering for worship throughout all the congregations of the true Church will have Adoration, Confession, Thanksgiving and Supplication. God's entire family, both Church Militant and Church Triumphant, gathers for one purpose - to worship and glorify God, our Creator, Redeemer, Counselor. As the Scriptures tell us,

⁶ All the nations of the world will turn and reverence God in truth; all will cast away their idols, which have deceitfully led them into error. ⁷ They will bless the God of the ages in righteousness. All the Israelites truly mindful of God, who are to be saved in those days, will be gathered together and will come to Jerusalem; in security will they dwell forever in the land of Abraham, which will be given to them. Those who love God sincerely will rejoice, but those who commit sin and wickedness will disappear completely from the land (**Tb 14:6-7**).

As part of worshiping the Lord God Almighty, we recite something called the "Lord's Prayer" or the "Our Father." According to Jesus' friends, he taught them this prayer as a simple way to talk to God (**Lk 11:1-13**). It has all the parts of worship: Adoration, Confession, Thanksgiving and Supplication. There is a real comfort from the Holy Spirit in knowing that God's family everywhere is praying together as one person, united by words which sum up the whole Gospel.

The Lord's Prayer as found in the Gospel of Matthew is the most commonly used in modern liturgies. It reads:
"Our Father in heaven,
hallowed be your name.
10 Your kingdom come,
your will be done,
    on earth as it is in heaven.
11 Give us this day our daily bread,
12 and forgive us our debts,
    as we also have forgiven our debtors.
13 And lead us not into temptation,
    but deliver us from evil" (**Mt 6:9-13**).

When we see how magnificent and awesome the world around us is, our hearts naturally turn to adoration for the God who created the universe. That's the whole reason God created us - to enjoy living in the world and be thankful to the one who created it. Worries and cares of the moment will seem less important when realizing how amazing God is and how much he loves his creation.

Adoration of God reminds us of who he is and of who it is that loves and cares for us. We are reminded by the Scriptures that
33 All the works of the Lord are good.
He will supply every need in its time.
34 No one can say, "This is worse than that,"
for they will all be well approved in their time.
35 Now with all your hearts and voices, sing praises
and bless the Lord's name! (**Sir 39:33-35**)

When we realize how big God is, we become aware of how small we are. We realize that we have not lived as we could have. No one can by themselves. Remember, because of sin, we all have let others down, let ourselves down, but mostly importantly, we have let God down (**Rm 3:20**).

In confession, you talk to God about these things, asking for his forgiveness. We all flub things; we all fail; we all fall. Talking to God about our flaws is comforting and relaxing. There is no need to pretend because God loved us before we were born and knows all our faults (**Is 44:24**). God is merciful and God forgives us no matter how many times we fail, when we are truly sorry (**Ps 51:16-17**). Scripture assures us that we should not be ashamed to confess our shortcomings, saying, *"Do not be ashamed to acknowledge your sins, and do not struggle against a rushing stream"* (**Sir 4:26**).

Thanksgiving is joyous praise of God. Gratitude and joy are closely related. When we think about what God has done - for us, for others, or throughout history - and think about receiving His forgiveness for our sins, then giving thanks is a very natural thing to do.

Many of the Psalms are prayers of thanksgiving, such as *"Give thanks to the LORD, for he is good; his love endures forever"* (**Ps 118:1,29**). And beyond the Psalms, Scriptures confirm it is right and good to give thanks to God,

27 For that which was not destroyed by fire,
   melted away when it was simply warmed by a faint sunbeam,
28 that it might be known that we must rise before the sun to give you thanks,
   and must pray to you at the dawning of the light;

Supplication is when we ask God for what we need. Sometimes, supplication is requesting for God to do something, either for yourself or somebody else. God is a loving father who cares for you very much. So don't be afraid to ask God for help when you're worried or upset about something. He will always make sure that you have what you need. But remember, just because you want something doesn't mean you need it.

God will always work things out in your best interest. And sometimes, just talking to God about things is help enough (**Mt 7:7**). The Apostle Paul encourages believers to offer prayers of supplication to God: "*do not be anxious about anything, but in everything by prayer and supplication with thanksgiving let your requests be made known to God*" (**Php 4:6**). St. Paul even implicitly endorsed the practice of "prayer requests" (**Col 4:3, 1Th 5:25, Rm 15:30-33**).

In the modern Church era, there is a part of prayer life that is as contentious as the practice of baptism. That controversy centers on the prayer requests to those Christians in the Church Triumphant. Such prayer requests to the Christians in the Church Triumphant were never a controversy in the first 1500 years of the Church.

The prayer requests to the Church Triumphant is but one tool in the toolbox of faith - one of many tools - that may or may not be used as the believer sees fit for their walk of faith. Such prayers have been part of the Church since its beginning, as demonstrated by the ongoing witness of the Church of Antioch - the first Christian

Church outside of Jerusalem.

We're told in Scripture that the prayers of the faithful go up to God by the hand of an intermediary other than Christ (**Rv 8:4**). Even in the time of the Old Covenant we find Saul sought the guidance of the deceased prophet Samuel. Saul's sin wasn't that he sought Samuel's guidance but how he went about it (**1Sm 28:11-20, Sir 46:20**).

During the Maccabean Revolt against the Seleucid Empire, the Jewish High Priest Onias sought (and received) the help of the deceased prophet Jeremiah to defeat the enemy of God's people (**2Mc 15:14-17**).

Additionally, the Jewish people have observed the tradition of asking for third-party intercession for a very long time in their petitions for the prophet Elijah's help in times of trouble during their Passover observances.

Perhaps the most famous modern example of a prayer request to the brethren of the Church Triumphant happened in Memphis. In the 1950s, Danny Thomas started raising funds for the children's hospital as a fulfillment of a vow he made to St. Jude - patron saint of lost causes. Mr. Thomas sought St. Jude's assistance for making a successful career, vowing "Show me my way in life and I will build you a shrine." And the rest, as they say, is history.

Are we going to be like the Pharisees (**Mt 12:24**) and say that Mr. Thomas' success and subsequent fulfillment of the promise was the work of Satan in order to deceive people, or that the Holy Spirit didn't have a hand in it? Jesus himself said that doing so was the unforgivable sin (**Mt 12:31-32**).

Finally, to say that **Jn 14:13** speaks against petitions to St. Paul for prayer and guidance is to also say that it speaks against petitions, or "Prayer Requests", to Christians sitting in the pews of the earthly congregation.

St. Paul is living even now in the presence of God, so asking for him to pray for someone by name to God is no different than me asking for you to do the same. And just think how much further our prayers are amplified by not only our small earthly congregation but also by the vast heavenly congregation.

God works all things for the good of those who love him (**Rm 8:28**). So what is the "good" that comes from prayer requests to all the saints - not just those in the Church Militant? Praying specific petitions to God on behalf of others gives us a glimpse of what God deals with on a much greater scale. Praying specific petitions for others helps every soul progress in the eternal process of becoming like Jesus - becoming less self-centered.

There were many issues that at times divided the various congregations of the Early Church. Such issues were discussed and decided at the several ecumenical councils. But "Intercession of the Saints" was never an issue discussed at those councils. If it was something that was introduced later by one of the early congregations, then the other congregations would have surely objected - just as the Eastern churches objected regarding "Purgatory" and "Indulgences".

And as part of God's family, we are called to include all of the family in our worship and prayers, even those who are part of the Church Triumphant, for Scripture tells us

29 With all your soul fear God
   and revere his priests.
30 With all your strength love your Maker
   and do not neglect his ministers.
31 Honor God and respect the priest;
   give him his portion as you have been commanded:
   First fruits and contributions,
   his portion of victims and holy offerings.
32 To the poor also extend your hand,
   that your blessing may be complete.
33 Give your gift to all the living,
   and do not withhold your kindness from the dead (**Sir 7:29-33**)

As people get older and more experienced, their relationships with friends and family change. As babies, we were pretty much dependent on mom for everything. But as we got older, we would get up in the morning and go to school by ourselves. When we were younger, we couldn't get dressed by ourselves. In the same way, God's family has come to understand God differently over time.

God hasn't changed, but the Church's understanding of him has. A lot. And as time has gone on, the Holy Spirit has taught us those things God wants us to know to be more like Jesus. It is as St. Paul says in Scripture, *9 For we know in part and we prophesy in part, 10 but when the perfect comes, the partial will pass away. 11 When I was a child, I spoke like a child, I thought like a child, I reasoned like a child. When I became a man, I gave up childish ways. 12 For now we see in a mirror dimly, but then face to face. Now I know in part; then I shall know fully, even as I have been fully known* (**1Cor 13:9-12**).

Before he was crucified, Jesus told us that he had so much more to teach us. Jesus promised us that the Holy Spirit would teach us more as we are ready (**Jn 16:12–**

14). It is because of this promise that Jesus gave us the flexibility to adjust our ordinances in accordance with experience and knowledge via the *Power of the Keys* (**Mt 16:19, Mt 18:18, Jn 20:23**).

That's why Jesus also told his friends that they needed to be ready to change their expectations of how believers are supposed to behave. It is through the Holy Spirit that God's family learns to see injustice where it first saw justice. It is through the "Power of the Keys" that the Church teaches all believers what the Holy Spirit reveals.

It is because of the Power of the Keys that Christians are not required to be circumcised as it was under the Torah (**Lv 12:3**). It is because of the Power of the Keys that Christians do not sin by eating shellfish (**Ac 10:15**), which is an abomination before the Lord under the Torah (**Lv 11:10–12**). It is by the Power of the Keys that slavery, which was acceptable under the Torah (**Ex 21:1–10**), is now seen by Christians today as an abomination. It is because of the Power of the Keys that Christians no longer execute witches even though the Old Covenant demands it (**Ex 22:18**). It is through the Power of the Keys that Christians are not required to observe the Sabbath on Saturday (or any particular day) even though the Old Covenant demands that as well (**Ex 20:8–11**).

Would anyone honestly consider it to be Christian to bash the heads of babies in with rocks (**Ps 137:9**)? Or how about asking God to *never* forgive our enemies (**Ps 69:25-28**)? In **Ps 109**, the *inspired* author prays for the death of his enemy; that the enemy's children be beggars and that no one take pity on them; that his enemy's parents never have their sins forgiven (**Ps 109:6-15**).

And what about Samuel's killing of Agag? Consider the fact that Samuel, that prophet of God and last judge of Israel, condemned Saul for sparing the lives of babies and NOT committing genocide by sparing the Kenites (**1Sm:1-34**). Jesus taught us that we should love our enemies - not kill them (**Mt 5:43-48**).

In the 17th Century (and the centuries before), people accused of being witches were killed because the Church believed that God wanted witches to be killed (**Ex 22:18**). Because of this belief, a woman named Alice Lake was hanged in Massachusetts for being a witch in about 1651.

Why did they believe she was a witch? Because she saw her child who had died as a baby in a dream. This was 40 years before the infamous Salem Witch Trials. The good news for the Church is that because of the Power of the Keys, and through the revelation of the Holy Spirit, we no longer kill people accused of being witches.

Abraham Lincoln was the President who stood up to end slavery in the United States. When Lincoln was younger, he saw nothing wrong with slavery. But Lincoln was convinced by the Holy Spirit to speak out against slavery. However, when Lincoln was president there were some Church leaders who believed that God approved of slavery.

Deceived by Satan, they taught that God never condemned slavery in the Bible (**Ex 21:1–10**). But because the Holy Spirit opened their eyes to the truth, other Christian leaders taught that even though the Bible doesn't say anything against it, slavery is still immoral. Because of the Power of the Keys, and through the revelation of the Holy Spirit, slavery is now revealed by God to be antichrist.

Back in St. Paul's day, it was the custom among Romans, Greeks and Jews that women were *"seen but not heard"*. In fact, Paul writes that women should be kept out of the limelight and from positions of apostolic authority (**1Cor 14:34–35, 1Tm 2:11–14**). But in our contemporary times, we have seen how antichrist such attitudes are. It is time that all Christians submit themselves to the Power of the Keys and acknowledge how wrongheaded such misogyny really is.

Jesus was killed on a cross. He was killed by the government. For centuries, leaders of God's family had more people killed by the government. But now, many Christians know this is wrong because Jesus said that the person without sin should do the killing (**Jn 8:7-11**). And since no one is without sin, Christians know the government should never kill people as punishment (**Ecc 7:20, Rm 3:10**).

St. John even tells us that we deceive ourselves if we say that we are without sin (**1Jn 1:8**). It is because of the Power of the Keys, and through the revelation of the Holy Spirit, that Christians know that the death penalty is antichrist and not biblical.

Unfortunately, as with the issue of slavery, because of Satan's continued deception, not every Church leader in our country agrees with that. Some feel that because the Bible says God gives the authority to punish (**Rm 13:4**), it's okay to kill for breaking the law - even though lesser penalties like lifetime sentences in prison are more just and can be remedied when mistakes are made.

Such attitude ignores the many cases in this country where a person is proven innocent *AFTER* they've been executed. Such unmerciful rigid attitude overlooks what Jesus said. Such attitude ignores the mercy and justice that the Holy Spirit calls all believers in God's family to stand for. Scripture tells us "*Anyone who responds to others with acts of kindness is thinking of the future, because he will find help if he ever falls on hard times*" (**Sir 3:31**). How exactly does the State give life back once it has been taken by mistake? It can't - only God can.

It's high time for all Christians to use the Power of the Keys and stop fighting the findings of science. For over 500 years, many earthly congregations have resisted science as "anti-Christian". John Calvin and Martin Luther even went so far as to condemn Copernicus as a fool and heretic "deceived by Satan" for his discovery that the Earth goes around the Sun and NOT vice versa.

This was an outrageous sacrilege in the eyes of the Reformers - the same Reformers who called themselves "Divines" and sliced and diced the Holy Scriptures held as inspired by the Orthodox Churches for no other reason than to side with the same Jews who had rejected the Christ.

In Genesis, we read "*male and female he created them*" (**Gn 1:27**). However in today's modern world, science has discovered this is not the case 100% of the time. Approximately 1 in 2000 births is what is referred to as "intersex" (formerly known as "hermaphrodite") where the individual is technically *both* male *and* female genetically speaking. I've been told that there are as many intersex individuals as there are redheads.

In many of today's Christian Churches, such intersex individuals are not allowed to marry because the strict interpretation of "the Law". For an intersex individual to marry, it is a case of "male marrying male" or "female marrying female," no matter who they chose to marry. Such hardheartedness ignores that the scriptures tell us that it is not good for us to be alone, without a family of our own (**Gn 2:18**).

The time has come for all Christians to let go of the Old Covenant, including the Ten Commandments, which Christ fulfilled and from which Christians have been released (**Rm 7:4-7**). It is time for all Christians to stop rejecting the New Covenant which the Christ established by his divine authority, superseding the Old Covenant (**Jer 31:31–34**).

One Baptism

Nicene Creed: *I confess one baptism*

1Cor 12:13, Ga 3:27, Ep 4:5

In the modern Church era, there is perhaps no issue as contentious as baptism. There are mainly three issues that divide otherwise well-meaning Christians. The first controversy is regarding "Baptism by Affusion".

The 2004 edition of the <u>Oxford Dictionary of the Bible</u> says "*Archaeological evidence from the early centuries shows that baptism was sometimes administered by submersion or immersion... but also by affusion from a vessel when water was poured on the candidate's head...*"

Volume 1 of the 2006 edition of <u>The Cambridge History of Christianity</u> (Pg 160-161) also concludes from the archaeological evidence that pouring water three times over the head was a frequent arrangement.

It is interesting to also note that "*Many – if not most – surviving baptismal fonts are too shallow to have allowed submersion. In addition, a significant number of depictions show baptismal water being poured over the candidate's head (affusion), either from a waterfall, an orb or some kind of liturgical vessel.*" - according to <u>Living Water: Images, Symbols, and Settings of Early Christian Baptism</u> (Pg 137).

<u>Eerdman's Dictionary of the Bible</u> (Pg 148), also casts doubt on "the usual assumption that all NT baptisms were by immersion", stating that some early baptisteries were deep enough to stand in but not broad enough to lie down in, and even mentioning that ancient representations of Christ at his baptism show him standing in waist-deep water.

There are at least two instances in the New Testament where the Greek verb *baptizo* is used outside the context of Christian baptism - **Mk 7:3–4** and **Lk 11:38**. One speaks of how the Pharisees do not eat unless they "wash their hands" thoroughly, and, after coming from the market place, do not eat unless they "wash themselves" (literally, "baptize themselves"). The other tells how a Pharisee, at whose house Jesus ate, "was astonished to see that he did not first wash himself" (literally, "baptize himself") before dinner. These two passages clearly show that the word *baptizo* in the New

Testament cannot be assumed to mean "immerse".

The only reference in the New Testament to Christian baptism being administered in the open is in **Acts**. The actions of "going down into the water" and "coming up out of the water" are ascribed to both the baptizer and the baptized, and therefore do not necessarily involve immersion in the water (**Ac 8:38-39**). Doesn't the passage say that Philip went into the water and came out of it as well as the eunuch? They *both* went in and they *both* came out. If this passage proves that the eunuch was immersed, then it also shows that Philip was immersed - which is not really plausible.

The recorded stories of various martyrs show that many were baptized while awaiting martyrdom in prison where immersion would have been impossible. But the most commonly noted use for affusion was for ill or dying people who could not rise from their beds. It consequently became known as "baptism of the sick".

A common practice in the fourth century was Christians putting off baptism until the last moment, with people enrolling as catachumens but not being baptized for years or decades by this "baptism of the sick". Even though the practice was decried at the time, the intent of such criticism was not to promote immersion baptism, but to refrain from needlessly delaying baptism like Augustine did. Even Augustine chastised himself for putting it off.

The earliest known manual for Christian belief, the earliest "catechism", known as the Didache, says thus about baptism:

7:1 But concerning baptism, thus shall ye baptize.
7:2 Having first recited all these things, baptize {in the name of the

*Father and of the Son and of the Holy Spirit} in living (running)
water.
7:3 But if thou hast not living water, then baptize in other water;
7:4 and if thou art not able in cold, then in warm.
7:5 But if thou hast neither, then pour water on the head thrice in
the name of the Father and of the Son and of the Holy Spirit.*

The Didache is part of the Christian writings known as
the Apostolic Fathers. In the Early Church it was
considered by some Church Fathers to be an inspired
part of the New Testament. Although in the end, it was
not accepted into the New Testament canon by the
Church at large. However, the Ethiopian Orthodox
Church includes the Didascalia, a work which draws on
the Didache, in its "broader canon".

Finally, baptism by affusion was never a controversy in
the first 1500 years of the Church. I said before that
there were many, many issues that at times divided the
various congregations of the Early Church. Such issues
were discussed and decided at the several ecumenical
councils.

Baptism by affusion was never an issue discussed at
those councils. As with prayer requests to the Church
Triumphant, if affusion was something introduced later
by one of the early congregations, then the others would
have objected - just as the Eastern churches objected
regarding "Purgatory" and "Indulgences".

The second controversy raised by those Christians
arguing for "Immersion-only" regards "Infant Baptism".
As with Baptism by Affusion, Infant Baptism was never
a controversy in the first 1500 years of the Holy Church
and never an issue discussed at the Ecumenical Councils
of the Early Church. If Infant Baptism was something

introduced later by one of the early congregations then the other congregations would have objected. None did. It was not even an issue until the schismatic Zwingli and his followers made it an issue in the 1500s.

Baptism is the rite/sign of the adoption of the Christian into God's family. We're told by Scripture that
18 For Christ also suffered once for sins, the righteous for the unrighteous, to bring you to God. He was put to death in the body but made alive in the Spirit. 19 After being made alive, he went and made proclamation to the imprisoned spirits— 20 to those who were disobedient long ago when God waited patiently in the days of Noah while the ark was being built. In it only a few people, eight in all, were saved through water, 21 and this water symbolizes baptism that now saves you also—not the removal of dirt from the body but the pledge of a clear conscience toward God. It saves you by the resurrection of Jesus Christ, 22 who has gone into heaven and is at God's right hand—with angels, authorities and powers in submission to him (**1Pt 3:18-22**).

Just as baptism is the sign of adoption into God's family for the Christian, circumcision is the sign of adoption into God's family for the Children of Abraham. Regarding circumcision, Scripture tells us,
9 God said to Abraham: For your part, you and your descendants after you must keep my covenant throughout the ages. 10 This is the covenant between me and you and your descendants after you that you must keep: every male among you shall be circumcised. 11 Circumcise the flesh of your foreskin. That will be the sign of the covenant between me and you (**Gn 17:9-11**).

Because circumcision is the rite/sign of adoption of the Jew into God's family, God commanded that all male children be circumcised eight days after they are born - not eight days after they make a profession/confession of faith. Notice that there is no requirement for any profession of faith or other statement of belief. What God required was that "*On the eighth day the boy is to be circumcised"* (**Lv 12:3**).

Clearly, God intended for children, even infants, to be included in his family, his covenant. Which is why *"Jesus said, Let the children come to me, and do not prevent them; for the kingdom of heaven belongs to such as these"* (**Mt 19:14**).

Baptism by water is the outward action which demonstrates how the Holy Spirit comes into our lives. Just as the Church pours water onto the new child of God's family, the Holy Spirit pours forth onto the soul, circumcising the heart (**Dt 30:6, Col 2:11-12**).

One prominent example of the the Holy Spirit working through infants is when Mary, mother of Jesus, went to visit her cousin, Elizabeth, after the Annunciation by the angel, Gabriel (**Lk 1:41-45**). Baptism of the Spirit is like the pouring of that water, for Scripture tells us
24 Listen to me, my son, and take my advice,
   and apply your mind to my words,
25 While I pour out my spirit by measure
   and impart knowledge with care. (**Sir 16:24-25**)
and also
That is why the Lord is patient with them
   and pours out his mercy on them. (**Sir 18:11**)
Let us not reject those who God clearly includes in his family.

The third issue regarding baptism is the idea of "re-baptism" - getting baptised again. It is possible to be circumcised only once and since baptism is to Christians what circumcision is to the Old Covenant (**Col 2:11-13**), there is never a need for Christians to get baptised more than once, no matter how badly they feel they've sinned. The Prodigal Son wasn't re-adopted into his family - even when separated by sin, he was still considered part of the family by his father (**Lk 15:11-32**).

Forgiveness of Sin

Apostles' Creed: *The forgiveness of sins,*

Nicene Creed: *for the forgiveness of sins*

Neh 9:17, Mk 11:26, Mt 6:12-15, Lk 6:37-38, Ac 22:16, Col 1:13-14, 2:12-14, Ep 1:7

First, let's consider what sin is. The Greek word for sin is "αμαρτια". Breaking it down, there is the prefix "α-" which means absence (apathy vs sympathy) and there is the word "μαρτια" which means witness (where we get the word "martyr"). So essentially, sin means to act without witness, or regard, for God.

Let's also consider **Jn 13:34–35** which says *"A new commandment I give to you, that you love one another. Just as I have loved you, you also love one another. By this everyone will know that you are my disciples, if you have love for one another."* This passage goes hand-in-hand with **Mt 22:36–40** which says, *"Teacher, which is the greatest commandment in the Law? Jesus replied: Love the Lord your God with all your heart and with all your soul and with all your mind. This is the first and greatest commandment. And the second is like it: Love your neighbor as yourself. All the Law and the Prophets hang on these two commandments."*

Jesus told us that he came to fulfill the Old Covenant, not to negate it (**Mt 5:17–20**). What does that mean? When the terms of a contract are fulfilled, the parties to the contract are no longer obligated to perform under the terms of that contract (or covenant). Would you continue to send money to a bank on a loan that has been paid in full (fullfilled)?

According to **Rm 7:4-7,** because the Christ fulfilled the Old Covenant, we have been released from its obligations. That is is why Paul says that all things are lawful (**1Cor 10:23, 1Cor 6:12, Rm 14:14, Tit 1:5**). We are free to do what we will.

Does this mean that there is no sin? Not in the least! In fulfilling the Old Contract, Jesus established a New Covenant (**Heb 8:8, Lk 22:20**). The prophet Jeremiah even tells us that the New Covenant will be written on our hearts - not with inanimate letters on dead leaves (**Jer 31:31**).

The first and greatest commandment is to love God above all else; the second commandment is to love others as we love ourselves (**Mt 22:36–40**). He even reiterated the second command at the last supper (**Jn 13:34**). The takeaway from this is that acting with a charitable heart is the only law that rules over Christians (**Gal 5:6**). Jesus promised us that his yoke would be easy, his burden light (**Mt 11:28–30**).

Anytime we don't do the right thing and disobey the Law of God written on our heart by the Holy Spirit (**Heb 10:16**), that is when we sin - whenever we fail to act with a charitable heart. Because of our selfish sinful nature, it's not easy to act out of love. That's what the sin of Sodom was about - it had nothing to do with sex and everything to do with being greedy, selfish, and uncaring (**Ek 16:49–50**). That is the sin that the nation of Israel was guilty of. And that was the lesson Jesus taught us in the parable of the sheep and the goats (**Mt 25:31–46**). Those who were cast out were condemned to eternal torment not for anything they did, but for what they *didn't* do.

So what shall we do when we realize we've sinned? We

are told what we need to do in the Scriptures:

*24 But to the penitent he provides a way back
    and encourages those who are losing hope!
25 Turn back to the Lord and give up your sins,
    pray before him and make your offenses few.
26 Turn again to the Most High and away from iniquity,
    and hate intensely what he loathes.* (**Sir 17:24-26**)

Part of acting with a charitable heart means forgiving others for the wrongs they commit against us. Scripture tells us,

*2 Forgive your neighbor the wrong done to you;
    then when you pray, your own sins will be forgiven.
3 Does anyone nourish anger against another
    and expect healing from the LORD?
4 Can one refuse mercy to a sinner like oneself,
    yet seek pardon for one's own sins?* (**Sir 28:2-4**)

When we refuse to forgive others, we are searing our heart in anger, not love. And that indignant anger really stems from pride. Our refusal to forgive becomes resentment, telling ourselves "*How dare that so-and-so do such a thing to me!!*" We forget that Jesus wasn't nailed to the cross for anything he did, but for what YOU did (and what I did.) When we refuse to forgive, bitterness ensues and hardens our hearts (**Heb 12:15**). An unforgiving heart reveals how we regard Jesus (**Jn 14:24**).

But when we truly regret and repent of our uncharitable attitude, God is merciful and just to forgive us - even when we keep screwing up and keep doing the same thing over and over (like giving in to an addiction.) God knows our hearts and he knows when we're sincere and when we aren't. We're told in Scripture:

*29 How great is the mercy of the Lord,
    and his forgiveness for those who return to him!*

30 For not everything is within human reach,
  since human beings are not immortal. (**Sir 17:29-30**)
and again:
For the Lord is compassionate and merciful;
  forgives sins and saves in time of trouble. (**Sir 2:11**)

Resurrection of the Body

Apostles' Creed: *The resurrection of the body,*

Nicene Creed: *and I look forward to the resurrection of the dead*

Ecc 12:7, Mt 22:31-32, Mk 12:18-27, Lk 20:27-37, Rm 6:4-5, 8:23, 1Cor 15:38-56, 2Cor 4:14, 1Th 4:16

When a person dies, the soul is separated from the body. Body and soul remain separated until the Second Coming. At the final judgment, everyone will stand before Jesus as a full person, with body and soul. For this to happen, the body must be resurrected and be united with the soul. This happens just before the final judgment. As Scripture tells us:

13 Like clay in the hands of a potter,
  to be molded according to his pleasure,
So are people in the hands of their Maker,
  to be dealt with as he decides.
14 As evil contrasts with good, and death with life,
  so are sinners in contrast with the godly. (**Sir 33:13-14**)

Because of the corruption of the world due to sin, we need incorruptible bodies to enjoy living in the presence of God. Your resurrected body will be different from the way it is now. It won't get sick or broken. It will be spiritual and incorruptible, and you will live forever. But it will still be your body and everyone will still know it's you. The resurrected body will be immortal, living forever (**1Cor 15:44**).

Those who are still alive when Jesus returns will also be changed - their bodies, like those of the dead, will be spiritual and made immortal. And each body will have its own individuality. It is a bit exciting to think about the fact that our new bodies will be identical in form to the glorious body of the resurrected Jesus, no longer suffering the consequence of sin (**1Cor 15:51-53**).

It is only by power of God-Creator that Jesus was resurrected. And it is only by the power of the resurrected God-Redeemer that all mankind will be resurrected at the Second Coming. Sin brought the corruption of physical death, and the eternal torment of the Second Death, which is the timeout that lasts forever. But it is the resurrection that takes away that sin and the corruption and death that it brings (**1Cor 15:21-22**).

God-Redeemer gives us life through His death on the Cross and His Resurrection. To understand what it means to be given life, it is important to understand the death we have been born into. Because of sin, man's nature was changed. Even though we still have the image of God in us (**Gn 1:26-27**), it has become corrupted. This spiritual corruption makes our body more subject to decay after death. But because the Christ redeems us, that image is restored (**Col 3:10**).

We are born into that spiritual corruption with an inherited tendency or inclination toward sin. All of us sin, and so we deserve the consequences of sin which is eternal timeout separated from God. So a perfect, blameless sacrifice was needed - a man who is without sin - in order to destroy the consequences of sin (**1Cor 15:55-57**). That's why Jesus was born. God-Redeemer came into the world to restore what was lost (**Gal 1:4**).

But Jesus did even more than that. He not only restored us, Jesus makes it possible for us to become what people were supposed to be if there had never been sin in the first place. By taking on our sins, as our scapegoat, we are freed from the corruption brought by those sins (**1Cor 5:21**). Through his death on the cross and through his resurrection, Jesus heals us and gives us life.

At the time of the Second Coming the bodies of human beings will be resurrected. This will be the Second Resurrection. We take part in the First Resurrection through Baptism (**1Pt 3:21**) and Holy Communion (**1Cor 11:26**), while the Second Resurrection is at Christ's Second Coming. With the resurrection of the dead and the final judgment, death is abolished. The whole human being will experience either eternal well-being or eternal distress.

The end of the world means change and finality and not some sort of great cataclysm. When he comes again, Jesus will bring a new Heaven and a new Earth that will last forever. It could happen 1,000,000 years in the future or more. It could be less. Only God the Father knows exactly when (**Mt 24:36**).

When a person dies, their spirit/soul is immediately removed from the constraints of time and space of the 3-dimensional creation. Where the spirit/soul goes is outside of time. In terms of our 3-dimensional world, we go immediately to the time of the Second Coming and are immediately resurrected with a new spiritual body

(**Php 3:17-21**). It will seem as if we traveled in Time to whenever the Second Coming actually happens. It's the sort of thing that you see in science fiction shows like "Dr. Who". Only that "void" outside the Universe is not a void at all - it's where God is.

Jesus' resurrection is a declaration of victory over death. With the Second Resurrection and the final judgment, death is abolished. Sin will disappear. Everyone will proceed to eternal union with God or eternal quarantine, separated from God because of sin (**Mt 25:31-46**).

Life Everlasting

Apostles' Creed: *And the life everlasting. Amen*

Nicene Creed: *and the life of the world to come. Amen.*

Dn 12:2, Mt 25:31-33, Lk 16:22-23, Jn 5:28-29, Rm 6:22-23, Ga 6:7-8, Ti 3:5-7, 2Pt 3:13, Rv 21:1

Christ revealed to us that he will come to judge the living and the dead. Jesus said that he will separate human beings, as a shepherd separates the sheep from the goats, and the righteous will go "into eternal life" and the sinners "into everlasting punishment" (**Mt 25:46**). Another way Scripture puts it is,

16 Though the sweet fragrance of every sacrifice is a trifle,
 and the fat of all burnt offerings but little in your sight,
 one who fears the Lord is forever great.
17 "Woe to the nations that rise against my people!
 the Lord Almighty will requite them;
 in the day of judgment he will punish them:
He will send fire and worms into their flesh,
 and they will weep and suffer forever" (**Jdt 16:16-17**).

What God wanted in the beginning of creation is full

and eternal communion with mankind - what we call Heaven, or Paradise. The saints in Heaven are without sin; filled with the Spirit and in full communion with God - but not perfect. Only God is perfect. Jesus is God, so he is perfect.

But people are not perfect. When God created man, he saw that it was good - not perfect (**Gn 1:31**). We weren't created to be perfect. We were created to be in a continual process of becoming like God, but not to become God. As we are finite and God is infinite, the process of becoming like Jesus is never-ending - like pouring cereal into a bowl that keeps growing.

Everyone will see the glory of God, and from that perspective, we all have the same end. While everyone will certainly see the glory of God, the difference is that while the faithful will see the glory of God as sweetest light, the condemned will see the same glory of God as consuming fire, as fire that will burn them (**Heb 12:28**).

Seeing his glory and his Light, is something that will happen whether we want it or not. The task of the Church is to tell people that God exists; that at the Second Coming of Christ all of us will see God; and that God is revealed as either light or consuming fire. The Church is to prepare its members so that they see God as light - not fire.

We know that God loves the damned as much as the faithful. God wants all to be cured of sin, but not everyone accepts the vaccine that he offers. But to those who accept that medicine for sin, Scripture tells us,

15 Whoever obeys me will judge nations;
   whoever listens to me will dwell in my inmost
   chambers.

16 If they remain faithful, they will possess me;
   their descendants too will inherit me (**Sir 4:15-16**).

In what way are the people in God's Family being prepared? By going from being self-centered to being "other-centered". It is pride that causes us to turn from God, thinking that we are wiser. So it is pride that must be put in proper perspective. The whole reason that God-Redeemer became a man is to show us how to put away our pride. Scripture says,

8 They shall judge nations and rule over peoples,
   and the LORD shall be their King forever.
9 Those who trust in him shall understand truth,
   and the faithful shall abide with him in love:
Because grace and mercy are with his holy ones,
   and his care is with the elect (**Wi 3:8-9**).

When people in God's Family die the first physical death, they still remain a vital part of the Church. They are alive in the Lord and "registered in heaven". They worship and pray to God and inhabit His heavenly dwelling places (**Heb 12:22-24**).

God the Father, God the Son, God the Holy Spirit, the holy angels, and the saints enrolled in heaven are *all* present in that worship. In worship, God's Family in heaven is unceasing in praise and thanksgiving to God. There are numerous Scripture passages that describe worship in the Heavenly Realm. In one, we see worship in heaven through the eyes of the prophet Isaiah who lived about 700 years before Jesus became man.

When Isaiah was caught up into the heavenly dimension, he described what took place. He says, *"I saw the Lord sitting on a throne, high and lifted up, and the train of His robe filled the temple"*. Present as well were the seraphim singing: *"Holy, Holy, Holy is the Lord of hosts; The whole earth is full of His glory*". Isaiah described the building in detail.

One of the seraphim took a set of tongs and removed a coal from the altar. He touched the coal to Isaiah's lips, saying, *"Behold this has touched your lips, your iniquity is taken away, and your sin is purged"*. The connection between Isaiah's vision and Holy Communion cannot be overlooked! Heavenly worship is the ultimate reality. Just as Isaiah experienced the liturgy of heaven, so we also enter God's presence in heavenly worship, being joined to Christ and risen with him in the Heavenly Realm (**Is 6:1-6**).

Scripture tells of a "great cloud of witnesses" in the Heavenly Realm. These witnesses are the saints who have passed on to their rest. There is an innumerable company of angels. Because the world is so corrupted by sin, the Heavenly Realm will bring a New Heaven and New Earth (**Is 65:17-18**). In the Heavenly Realm are the general assembly and God's family in heaven - all the spirits of those with God's grace (**Heb 12:1-2**).

What does God mean by the Second Death? What is meant by the Eternal Fire? Hell is a permanent quarantine - a permanent spiritual separation from God. Hell will be a dark place just as those who rejected the miracles that Jesus performed right in front of them remained in a darkness of the mind, not filled with light. But that darkness is self-inflicted due to the state of the heart.

13 Like clay in the hands of a potter,
*   to be molded according to his pleasure,*
So are people in the hands of their Maker,
*   to be dealt with as he decides.*

Heaven and Hell do not exist from the point of view of God, but from the point of view of human beings. God loves everyone equally. He will send his grace to all, in the same way that he "... *makes his sun rise on the evil and on the good, and sends rain on the just and on the unjust*" (**Mt 5:45**).

But not everyone will accept God's grace in the same way. Some will see God as light and others will see God as fire. How many times have we heard from the skeptics as they reject God, "*If God really exists and is so good, then why does he allow 'bad thing X' to happen to good people?*"

Which is where "punishment" comes in - the unsaved will be punishing themselves due to their own choices. The Light of Jesus is the fiery torment that exists within the heart of the person who is spiritually separated from God, thereby creating a darkness in the mind - much like a clinically depressed person just cannot see the good things in their life because they are overwhelmed with inexplicable despair. There will be weeping and gnashing of teeth (**Lk 13:28**).

Think about people like medical doctors who don't have the saving grace of Jesus in their heart; who made their work their "all" instead of God. They will find themselves without purpose at the Second Coming since there won't be anymore sickness. The same goes for lawyers, politicians, accountants, garbage collectors, teachers, etc. Anyone who makes their "all" something other than God will have essentially wasted their entire lives and have nothing to show for it but a burning regret after the Resurrection. Scripture again tells us,

*10 But the wicked shall receive a punishment to match their
    thoughts,
    since they neglected righteousness and forsook the LORD.
11 For those who despise wisdom and instruction are
    doomed.
Vain is their hope, fruitless their labors,
    and worthless their works* (**Wi 3:10-11**).

The Glory of Christ, which is by nature from the Father, is paradise for those who have been cured of selfish love and being self-centered. However, that same glory is eternal fire for those who have chosen to refuse the vaccination for their selfishness. From this point of view, therefore, Christians agree with the most liberal people in the world.

No message can be more liberal than "We'll all go to the same place." It is a liberal practice to emphasize that God loves everyone equally: the condemned and the redeemed, the saved and the unsaved, angels and devils, good and bad, prostitutes and chaste. God loves all human beings equally, he loves everyone without distinction.

From God's point of view, God saves everyone. He wants the salvation of all human beings, and he has preordained salvation for all. Scripture tells us

*12 Great as his mercy is his punishment;
    he judges people, each according to their deeds.
13 Criminals do not escape with their plunder;
    the hope of the righteous, God never leaves unfulfilled.
14 Whoever does good has a reward;
    each receives according to their deeds.* (**Sir 16:12-14**)

Even Hell is salvation where the human being is preserved. But Hell is not Paradise because the one who is damned is unable to progress towards perfection. The conscience has been hardened, the heart has grown hard. The condemned remains so egotistic and self-centered that he cannot develop from selfishness to unselfishness. He is perfected in his selfishness.

It is not punishment from God's point of view, but punishment from the human point of view. Another way to think of Hell is as a "pit of despair":

Be like a father to orphans,
*   and take the place of a husband to widows.*
Then God will call you his child,
*   and he will be merciful to you and deliver you from the pit*
(**Sir 4:10**).
And for Jacob's son, Joseph, being thrown into a pit was salvation from those brothers who thought to kill him (**Gn 37:18-36**).

The man in the pit has remained uncured. Why? Because his heart needed to be cured and he did not accept treatment. Where does this treatment begin, how does it take place and how does a human being secure it? For God's family, the cure to sin begins here in this world.

Although its exact nature is not revealed by God, there will be some sort of separation between the saved and unsaved. Those who can't stand the Light of Jesus will try to get away from it, just as people will try to get away from a burning forest fire. The gates to Hell are locked from within the hearts of those who didn't accept the healing Grace of Jesus. It is written,

Some he blessed and exalted,
*   and some he sanctified and drew to himself.*
Others he cursed and brought low,
*   and expelled them from their place.* (**Sir 33:12**)

It will be an eternal quarantine, but just how it happens is unclear, and really none of my concern, nor the business of anybody else.

After the Resurrection, good stewardship will be our natural inclination, instead of sin. There won't be rude people selfishly wasting what God has given us. We will take care of God's creation as he intended for us in the first place. Giving thanks to God and enjoying his creation will be the order of the day.

God created the Heavens and the Earth in the first place. With the new Heaven and new Earth, we will be able to not only see the beauty of the creation, we will be able to see the full glory of God-Creator (**Rv 21:1-4**) bringing us full circle with the beginning (**Gn 1:1-31**). Amen.

About the Author

What is there to say? D. Joseph "Ren" Remington is a lifelong Christian who grew up in the jungles of Cedar Rapids, Iowa, and finds himself currently living in Memphis, TN, with his family. He enlisted in the U.S. military on his 17th birthday in 1983 and served for 10 years, receiving an honorable discharge on April 1, 1993. Ever since, he's been trying to keep his way as a civilian following that still-small voice of the Holy Spirit.

As a Christian, Ren is well-versed in Ecclesiastical History, History of the Bible, Koine Greek (Old and New Testaments) and enough Biblical Hebrew to be dangerous. Having also studied the Apostolic and Early Church Fathers, Ren feels that every Christian should read the Didache and the Shepherd of Hermas at least once in their lives.